Travels
with the
Evil Inclination

Also by Gershon Winkler

Magic of the Ordinary: Recovering the Shamanic in Judaism

The Way of the Boundary Crosser: An Introduction to Jewish Flexidoxy

Sacred Secrets: The Sanctity of Sex in Jewish Law and Lore

The Place Where You Are Standing is Holy: A Jewish Theology on Human Relationships

The Called Her Rebbe: The Maiden of Ludomir

The Soul of the Matter: A Jewish-Kabbalistic Perspective on the Human Soul Before, During, and After Life

Dybbuk

The Golem of Prague

I dedicate this book to my ancestors

who can now truly rest in peace,

for this personal exposé far surpasses theirs as

sensationalized in the Hebrew Scriptures.

Indeed, I have written this book in order to divert

attention away from perpetual readings

about their embarrassing exploits during their travels

with the Evil Inclination

by drawing attention to mine.

Far be it from me to be as brazen as to declare

that I have written a more fascinating book

than the Bible.

But fact is, I have.

Used to follow the letter of the law

The most Orthodox Jew you ever saw

Not one Halachah did I leave behind

'Til I crossed the line

'Til I crossed the line

I wore a yarmulka bigger than a hat

And my sins were smaller than a gnat

I was what you call the yeshiva kind

'Til I crossed the line

'Til I crossed the line

I tore toilet paper Friday afternoons

Felt guilty humming irreligious tunes

I fought hard to keep lewd thoughts out of my mind

'Til I crossed the line

'Til I crossed the line

ঙ্গ song: 1983

Acknowledgments

Thank you, Roger Kamenetz, for that annoying walk in upstate New York in 1999 during which you kept *nudnicking* me to write this book. Thank you, Dr. Carl Hammerschlag, for standing in the corner of my cabin patiently reading through Chapter Seven and then convincing me of the importance of writing Chapters One through Six as well. Thank you, David Carson, for making our transition here not only easy but warm and welcoming, and for introducing us to Native America. Thank you, Joel Ehrlich, for enabling our relocation to New Mexico which led to the unfolding of our dream life, and sustaining us until Bob Levin came along. Thank you, Bob, for coming along and inspiring the vision that became Walking Stick, and that catapulted me into a quality and venue of teaching that has benefited me deeply and that continues to benefit untold thousands across the globe. Thank you Abe and Eli Cordova for fixing our vehicles whenever they broke down, especially for that inventive new muffler that extended several feet and then turned sideways and upward and out. Thank you, Gzombor, for driving miles and miles at low speed on your tractor to pull our cars and trucks out of knee-deep mud and snow several times a week annually. Thank you, Anna, for coaching our kid on horseback and for your relentless data entry and effective administration of Walking Stick Foundation. Thank you, Aharonit, for interrupting dad while he was writing this book, by insisting that he watch you run up the cliff barefoot, or jump off a ledge, or dash between the cabin and the house in a record four seconds flat. Thank you, Richard Grossinger for having the *chutzpah* to publish this highly irreverent and obscene book, and thank you, Sarah Serafimidis its project editor, for your stamina and good humor as you persevered through the arduous process of its publication.

Finally, very special thanks to all the powerful women who helped me to evolve and who fought bravely and relentlessly to redeem me from the Evil Inclination. Thank you, Devorah, for what will always remain our private untold story, too wild for even contemporary cinema, and for your role in transitioning me through my initial meta-morphoses. Thank you, Jessica, for pulling away the cobwebs that clouded my aliveness, and sharing those important wilderness walks with me. Thank you, Megan, for introducing me to yet deeper places of love and passion within myself, and for boldly challenging my self-truth by compelling me in front of a mirror I'd always been afraid of looking into. Thank you, Elana, for holding that very same mirror steadily in front of me until I cried Uncle and faced fully some very important issues I might otherwise never have faced. Thank you, Rena, for that brief but incredibly wonderful taste of being so completely doted on by an amazingly loving heart and soul. And a huge huge thank you, Lakme, for loving me through thick and thin, and for sticking by me even through the most compromising moments of my strange life journey—because you believed in me through and through (and still do). Finally, thank you, Miriam, for your awesomeness; for bringing a dimension of magic to my life that I had never known before, not even dreamed possible—personally and professionally—leaving me with no gaps yet to be filled and no appetite for more.

To all of you, I am left speechless and can say only this: "Wow."

Table of Contents

Chapter One

Genesis

I was born in Denmark at the age of four. I came from a long line
of rabbis who traced their ancestry directly to Adam and Eve. Unlike
most people, I didn't come into the world by some biological cause
and effect. I deliberated in getting here. I hesitated at the door of the
womb, taking life step by step, inching my way into being-ness, questioning everything as I went along, often even considering the possibility of maybe going back, like maybe this wasn't a good idea after
all. I always believed in reincarnation, long before I studied about it
in the writings of melancholic medieval kabbalists.

All that aside, I was born in Denmark at the age of four.

Now, the story I am about to tell you is true. Only the names
have been changed to protect myself from libel suits and revenge. For
instance, I have decided to refer to my ex-wife as "Bryna," which
by chance also happens to be her real name, but that's purely coin-
cidental. I have also chosen to leave out references to specific relationships with all the women I've loved before who meandered in
and out my door, so as not to embarrass them and to avoid further
paternal claims. Also, I owe a lot of people money, so I'm not going
to mention _them_ in the story. In fact, I was initially going to write
this book under the pseudonym of George Bernard Shaw, which I

made up, but I decided that at fifty-four I'm too old for cowardice. And anyway, most of my creditors are dead. They died laughing when I promised them that I would pay them back. Others suffer from amnesia. They remember how much they are owed, but they don't remember by whom.

But what you are about to read is my story of theological dissolution and re-emergence, the story of my journey from being a nice, normal, ultra-Orthodox rabbi in New York to being an escaped, renegade, ultra-*Flexidox* rabbi yodeling his life away in the remote wilds of northwestern New Mexico, some 2,000 miles from the Second Avenue Deli and two hours from the nearest Jewish community.

Let me just point out that I'm not—God forbid—an anti-Semite. Some of my best friends are Jews. It isn't my fault that Jews don't live where I live. But this book is dedicated to all those *nudniks* who are always asking me what a nice Jewish boy like me is doing in the wilderness where no one can see me? I believe the question to be a valid one. After all, how is anyone going to know whether I'm keeping the commandments or not? It's true that God sees everything. But where I live, the trees and rocks are in the way.

Anyway, I was born in Denmark at the age of four. According to my parents, I was born in the same hospital bed that my father was born in, and delivered by the same midwife that my father was delivered by. In fact, this remarkable woman delivered all of *my* children, too, and my grandchildren.

It is also important to note that the year in which I was born, 1949, was no mediocre year. According to the Almanac for that year, NATO was also born in 1949. And there was an earthquake in Ecuador that killed six thousand people, a cyclone in India that claimed a thousand, and a typhoon in the Philippines that claimed yet another thousand. It was also the year that Mao Tse Tung took over China and painted her red, and the year the Israeli-Arab war ended in the aftermath of Israel's earlier War of Independence from Britain. It was the year Jerusalem got split into two, and Germany got split into two, too, along the infamous Berlin Wall. In 1949, William L.

Genesis

Dawson became the first African American to head a congressional committee, and Russia exploded her first Atom Bomb, ending America's monopoly on nuclear arms and launching the Cold War.

The Almanac also stated that the lifespan of a toad is thirty-six years, so ever since my thirty-sixth birthday I have stopped celebrating my birth and have instead begun celebrating the fact that I've outlived the toad by yet another year. But all of this is irrelevant to the story you are about to read, so please disregard it and continue.

In 1956, my parents decided to immigrate to the United States because Denmark lacked Jewish educational opportunities and anti-Semitism. In America, however, a Jewish child could receive a thorough Jewish education *and* be hated for it. I know this might sound facetious to some, but in all seriousness it seems to me that Jews were constantly searching for places to live where people hated them. Compare, for example, how many Jews have lived in mostly Jew-hating Christian Europe for close to eighteen centuries, to how many Jews have lived in, say, India or Bali or the Congo or Native America for so much as *one* century. Plainly put, my people seem to have chosen to establish their roots in countries bent on expelling them. The Hindus would have left us alone, so only a very few of us settled in Burma. The Cheyennes would have left us alone, the Australian aborigines wouldn't have burnt us at the stake for being Jewish, the people of the Amazon wouldn't have painted swastikas and epithets on our homes and synagogues, so we never lived anywhere near any of those people. So there you have it. I'm a rabbi. I know about these things. And that's why I've made it my policy to live nowhere near a Jewish community. Instead, I live where I *choose* to live. And ever since 1982, when I first moved out to the wilderness, I have not encountered a single anti-Semitic elk. And the few Jew-hating Hittites that I *did* encounter on occasion ended up in the ranks of my closest friends. More about that later, not now.

Anyway, I was born in Denmark at the age of four. And I emphasize being born in Denmark because being born in Denmark played a significant role in the process that ultimately catapulted me from

Orthodoxy to Flexidoxy. Had I been born in, say, Minsk or Pinsk, Brooklyn or Chicago, London or Jerusalem, I would have remained so normal that you'd have mistaken me for a regular rabbi. Instead, I was born in Denmark, and to this day whenever I perform a wedding, elderly Jewish women could be heard in the audience murmuring: "Dot's ah rabbi?" And this is all because I was born in Denmark. And don't ask me why. Maybe it's because Danes are humorous and brazen and unafraid to challenge authority, and they don't take life so seriously, and their national motto is "live and let live," as opposed to the national motto of the United States, which, as you know, is "add water and stir."

So I was born in Denmark at the age of four. I say "four" because quite frankly I have no recollection of having been around before then. So it's my word against that of my parents. And statistics often lie. And birth certificates could easily be forged. Four. Four, four, four.

For me, Four was an advantageous age at which to be born. My consciousness had developed at least sufficiently enough for me to remember four decades later what had happened back then. I remember, for instance, thinking of orange soda, which had just been invented at that time. I remember making in my pants and how awfully good that felt— the warmth, the softness, the magic in just letting go and filling up my pants with multi-textured bulk from inside of myself. To the nursery school teacher and my mother it was a smelly, yechy pooey mess. To me it was creative expression, a sharing and clearing from deep within my Inner Self, a spiritual experience I would miss sorely as I matured. And if you suppose that it's only I who feel this way about free-fall crapping, look at the latest fad amongst New Age health freaks, like those who engage in premeditated enemas. You know who you are. Sure, you claim it's for health purposes, homeopathically indicated, intended to clean out your colons and stuff. But deep down you know precisely why you do this shit. You're doing it because you miss terribly the experience I am talking about, of letting go completely, no holds barred, no preparation. It's the next best thing to doing the Primal Scream, but it's cheaper.

Four is also the age during which I remember first learning about God. My Danish father's Czechoslovakian mother was a saintly Jewish woman who covered herself down to her ankles, refusing to follow the fashions of the times because they were not *tz'niyus*, or modest. She was more Orthodox than Moses. Moses, as you know, wore shorts. But her Orthodoxy was anything but fanatical. She was a warm-hearted, compassionate woman we called *Mutti*, and when she spoke of God—whom she called *der eibershter* (German/Yiddish for "the One Above")—it was like she spoke of an intimate friend. And so I grew up with an image of God that was sweet, friendly, and Czechoslovakian, as opposed to rabid, psychotic, and American.

In other words, I lucked out with a positive start in life. My parents were wonderful, my childhood was wonderful, my religion was wonderful, my country was wonderful, my community was wonderful, and my God was easy. What could possibly go wrong?

But then we left Denmark and *Mutti* for New York City where I was thrown into a whirlwind of Orthodoxy I had never imagined, an Orthodoxy that was rigid, exacting, solemn, heavy, and draining. I missed my grandmother's lap, the greatest yeshiva I'd ever been to, and hated the new yeshiva I was now subjected to, where Judaism was about doing this and not doing that, rather than singing sweet lullabies to *der eibershter*. Now, however, *der eibershter* had turned sour on me, gone beserk, demanding I not tear toilet paper on the Sabbath, that I pray three times a day, that I wear a yarmulka on my head even when I'm playing, that I review my Torah studies after school, and so on. I didn't tear toilet paper on the Sabbath in Denmark, either. But the difference was that in Denmark God had a sense of humor about it. God and I would laugh about it if I *did* rip paper on the Sabbath, or if I prayed only *two* times a day, or if I didn't wear my yarmulka. In Denmark, it was an "oops, tee-hee"; in New York it was a "yikes! oy!"

Also, the New York deity frowned on the notion of Jewish kids playing with *non*-Jewish kids. Say hello and be polite but don't fraternize with them. In Denmark I played with non-Jewish kids all the time, lots of them. We all did. There was no taboo around it. We fraternized the hell out of them. My parents fraternized with the Jensens and the Hansens and the Petersens as if they were family. And they weren't even circumcised. But in America, all of that changed. We were now living in a community comprised mostly of Jews whose experiences with non-Jews had been purely dreadful, if not outright deadly. Now it became "us" and "them," an entirely new theology which I today call "reaction theology," arising not from the ancient texts and traditions of my people but from centuries of being kicked out, burned alive, pillaged, and blanketly persecuted for the crime of being Jewish.

Reaction theology was unheard of in Denmark. Heck, back as early as the sixteenth century, anti-Semitism was outright outlawed by the Danish Kingdom. Finished. And it stayed that way. So who knew from "us" and "them" theology? In fact, Denmark stood up as a nation in defense of its Jewish population during the Holocaust. More Danish *non*-Jews than Danish *Jews* were killed or shipped to concentration camps for hiding my people or aiding in their rescue during that tragic period. Such a country, that loved its Jews rather than hated them, was no place to raise Jewish kids, and so, again, we settled in America where we could at least be assured of *some* anti-Semitism.

It was going to take several decades before I would realize that the Judaism with which I'd been reared in the "yeshiva world" differed drastically from the Judaism intended by the ancient writ, upon which—ironically—the yeshiva world bases its dogma. I was to realize much later how the texts were the same but the voices of the texts were different. They were no longer the voices of Abraham or Judah or Moses or David or Isaiah or Hillel the Elder, or Rabbi Akiva, or Rami. They were instead the voices of latter-day saints who had been forged in the cauldron of centuries of religious suppression and persecution.

Judaism had over time evolved into a theology of fear and reaction rather than of celebration and faith. The voices of the ancients had been replaced by theological ventriloquism; voices of rigidity dubbing over voices of fluidity; cries of sternness outshouting whispers of compassion. The ancient rabbis taught (*Midrash Shir HaShirim Rabbah* 1:39) that Moses was kept from entering the Promised Land not because he disobeyed God and hit the rock instead of speaking to it, but because he raised his voice to the people and called them "infidels" (Numbers 20:8-12), and that Isaiah got his mouth scalded after he'd called us "a people of unclean lips" (Isaiah 6:5,7). The Second Temple, they taught, didn't fall because the people didn't keep the commandments, but because many of the rabbis of the time rendered their rulings strictly according to the letter of the law (Babylonian Talmud, *Baba Metzia* 86a). So not only was I to eventually discover that there is a major discrepancy between God and religion, but I was also to realize that the American Jewish Orthodoxy in which I was raised was more the product of recent history than of ancient theology. America, after all, had absorbed the remnants of a tragic European Jewish history.

Nevertheless, the kosher pizza was worth it.

And so I grew into this peculiar mode of being Jewish. I was to become very pious, very devout, and a meticulous adherent of every religious Jewish observance I could possibly get my hands on, short of offering sacrifices. I would go out of my way to do more than was actually required, and I'd pray so fervently that I was usually the last worshiper remaining in the synagogue after services. I would also write prolifically against rabbis like the very kind of rabbi I myself would later become, and I'd blame assimilation and intermarriage on those who would compromise Jewish tradition by deviating so much as a cubit from the only authorized form of that tradition: Orthodoxy. And not any kind of Orthodoxy, mind you, only the ultra-Orthodoxy of the yeshiva world. I would eventually become so zealous in my orthodoxy that even the bible itself smacked of heresy!

Let me calm down. I know I sometimes tend to exaggerate, and it confuses people. A lot of people don't know when I'm being serious and when I'm just playing. The truth is, neither do I. The truth is that I have tried so hard to be serious it's a joke. It never worked and never will. This is why I decided long ago not to affiliate myself with any denomination or rabbinic organization. I don't want to be a source of confusion to people who are seriously devoted to their movements. As for myself, the only movement that I have resigned to follow with devotion and regularity is the bowel movement.

Anyway, I was born in Denmark at the age of four. And I am about to share with you a story that will blow your mind reading it as it blew my mind living it. It is a story that I have been wanting to write since I was eleven years old, but since most of the events in the story had not yet happened, I had to wait patiently until I turned fifty-four. Lest you now think that my story ended at fifty-four, or that I—God forbid—died, let me remind you that my life goes on, as does the *story* of my life, only the danger and excitement of taking risks has lessened.

Now I'm settled in, settled in enough to be able to look back at this phenomenal true story that I am about to share with you if you would just bear with me. Don't get me wrong. I still take risks. I haven't become a patsy just because I'm fifty-four and a grandfather of six. It's just that the risks I take these days are more like, say, eating apple cores, joining book clubs, answering the telephone, and so on. Not exactly earth-shattering risks, but risks nonetheless.

But the story I am about to tell you is a story of some non-stop risk-taking, a series of which I engaged in once I took that fatal first step out of the ordinary, out of the safety of the pre-heated givens and definitions of my life. This is my story, and it might help you, too, to take chances that you might otherwise never have entertained, or at least entertain taking chances you might otherwise never have thought of. So as a disclaimer, the story you are about to read may be hazardous to your wealth, as it was to mine, and potentially corruptive of your purity and morals, as well as intrusive into your existential reality altogether.

Actually, writing this book is pretty risky in itself, because I have decided to tell my story no-holds-barred and straightforward even though this means recording incidents like trying to find a prostitute, or having lewd thoughts, or taking off my yarmulka, or saying dirty words, or eating food that wasn't labeled "kosher." I have included such obscene and startling episodes only where they are relevant to the message of this book, which is this: *some of the most tempting delicacies come wrapped so thoroughly that they are virtually impossible to access without making a fool of yourself in front of others as you struggle to rip, pull, cut, or bite off the wrapper.*

Anyone who's ever ordered a kosher airline meal knows exactly what I mean.

So this is my story. And I am taking such bold risks to tell it because I come from the People of the Book, the Book being the Jewish Bible. The Jewish Bible nonchalantly exposes such incredibly embarrassing moments in the lives of my ancestors that I feel I owe it to them to expose some of my own. You know very well what I'm talking about: Noah groveling naked in the dirt after a few beers (Genesis 20:21), David having an affair with Batsheba who is married to one of his captains (2 Samuel 11:2-4), Judah on his way to the village to visit a prostitute (Genesis 38:15-18), Leah bribing her sister Rachel for an extra turn in bed with their shared husband Jacob (Genesis 30:15-16). I mean, should I read the stories about my ancestors like some kind of holier-than-thou voyeur, and then camouflage my own story so that I should look better? Nonsense. You can't learn nearly as much from perfect stories about perfect people as you can from perfect stories about imperfect people. The Jewish bible is about the latter. And so is the story you are about to read.

I call this story "*Travels with the Evil Inclination*" because in essence that's what it's all about. In the yeshiva world, the Evil Inclination—or *yetzer ha-ra*—is the culprit responsible for talking you into doing stuff you shouldn't, kind of a seductive inner voice that dares you or lures you to venture outside the boundaries established for you by your religion, your morals, your community, your parents, or the cops. The *yetzer ha-ra* is a central figure in ancient and medieval Jewish theology, the forbidden fruit dangling temptingly from the tree in the middle of the garden that is off limits to you. And the great life challenge is to make it from the cradle to the grave without getting sidetracked by the Evil Inclination, who lies in wait for you every inch of your journey, sneaking up behind you when you least expect it, when you are least sensitive to it, and then—Pow!—you commit a boo-boo, a no-no, a sin. The trick in life is to run the gauntlet of the Evil Inclination and withstand its blows so that when you reach the other side, you might be bruised and exhausted from the struggle but your integrity is intact, your authenticity is in place, and your movie rentals have been dropped off along the way.

> In the time to come, the wicked shall be shown the Evil Inclination
> in the form of a strand of hair, and they shall then weep, declaring:
> "How could we not have overcome so small an obstacle?" The
> righteous, too, shall be shown the Evil Inclination, but in the form
> of a tall mountain, and they shall then weep, declaring: "How did
> we ever manage to overcome so huge an obstacle?"
>
> **Babylonian Talmud, Sukah 52a**

The ancient rabbis spoke only of a *yetzer*, an inclination, one that is neither good nor bad but is what you make it in the moment. But when the Church introduced dualism, the Jews adapted their theology accordingly in order to minimize their chances of getting burnt at the stake. All told, maybe two or three less Jews were set afire over the centuries as a reward for such theological adaptations. Nonetheless, "inclination" got replaced by "Evil Inclination." And it is about my travels with the Evil Inclination that I devote this book. None of my life processes and transformations could have happened without it. In fact, the rabbis of yore (a small city near Cleveland) taught that without the Evil Inclination, no one would build a house, get married, have kids (*Midrash B'reishet Rabbah*, Ch. 9) or, I might add, do laundry.

In the yeshiva world, when you're about to do something that smacks of forbiddenness, we say to you: "The *yetzer ha-ra* is getting to you. Don't give in." And the myriad teachings about this are so true and right on, as I will demonstrate to you in this book, replete with talmudic and midrashic sources interspersed throughout the story wherever they are relevant. This is an opportunity for you to study the ancient Jewish teachings about the Evil Inclination while reading about how I succumbed to it and also about how I employed it toward my journey of spiritual dissolution and re-emergence. In a way, this book is more than a story. It is a theology. And yet it breaks all the rules of theology, because it is a theology without portfolio written by a rabbi who not only is without portfolio, but who doesn't even know what theology actually means, let alone portfolio.

And now for the story. Really. No more sidetracking. No more divergence. No more straying on the tangent. No more avoiding the point. Here goes.

Actually, it is pretty much a Jewish tradition to venture off on the tangent. The Talmud, for instance, does this all the time. Like you'll have some heavy discussion about the laws of damages when suddenly they'll get into this rap about who's teacher has the bigger *pupick* (Babylonian Talmud, *Baba Metzia* 84a). But enough. On with my story, which I now share with you, and no one else, in great confidentiality.

I just want you to know one more thing. Nobody knows about this, about what happened to me, except for the elusive *Committee That Knows,* a mysterious band of Brooklyn rabbis who have been monitoring my every move since I strayed from the path in 1982, recording my every heretical deed and writ, clipping every article or Letter-to-the-Editor I've written since, and sending copies of them to my ex-publisher exclaiming: "Behold the wickedness of the writer whose works you continue to promote." For years I'd be summoned to New York to explain to my Orthodox Jewish publisher the accusations brought against me by the *Committee That Knows*. Eventually, I ran out of explanations and decided to look for other publishers. But the *Committee That Knows* still knows, and their spies continue to hide behind the bluffs and trees that surround our land, even as I write these very words. (Aha! I just spotted one outside my cabin window sneaking off to pee behind a rock.) My wife, bless her, even leaves snacks for them near the corral. Bless that woman.

Chapter Two

The Evil One

If the Evil Inclination confronts you,

drag it to the House of Study,

for there it is harmless.

If it be hard as a rock, it shall smatter;

if it be brazen as iron, it shall be

broken in pieces.

◦§ Babylonian Talmud, *Kidushin* 30b

I was born in Denmark at the age of four. And that's when I first met the Evil Inclination. He was sort of elusive at first, kind of checking me out as I matured, peeking out at me from behind the doorway leading to the long corridor leading to my room. At night I made sure my feet were covered at all times, lest he snatch me from my bed, feet first, and yank me into *yennervelt*, a Yiddish phrase for some kind of alternate reality you don't want to know about. And it worked. Covering up my feet worked. Once, only once, he almost got me. It was a really warm, humid night. We were in Brooklyn by then and I was about eight. No sooner had I kicked the blanket off my feet in my sleep when I was suddenly overcome by an overwhelming sense of sinister presence looming over me, shadowing my whole being. I awoke with a startle and reached desperately for the blanket, when he fled. He stayed away for a long time, probably meditating on how he could somehow get hold of me. It took him a mere three years to finally figure it out. By then I was eleven and my loins were on fire and I started fantasizing what it would feel like to touch Feigel Yontiff's ribs.

Travels with the Evil Inclination

> The Evil Inclination merges
> with a person from age thirteen and on.
> Others say from age ten and on.
>
> ✍ **Midrash Kohelet Rabbah, Ch. 4,**
> **and Tanchuma Breishet, Ch. 7**

So the Evil Inclination was no stranger to me in my childhood. He was the primary subject of my yeshiva upbringing. I had never heard of him in Denmark, but this side of the Atlantic he was something to be seriously reckoned with. See, there was the Evil Inclination and the good inclination, and they both were always trying to outdo each other to win my attention. Most of the time I would withdraw into myself while sitting in class at the yeshiva and doodle on the margins flanking the Talmudic text. I wasn't much into decision-making back then, just living, so I'd just sit there daydreaming and let the two bastards fight it out on their own. In the background, the *rebbe* or teacher would be flailing his arms excitedly as he tried to convey to us the absolute truth, especially the ancient rabbinic teachings about the Evil Inclination, or *yetzer ha-ra*. The *yetzer ha-ra*, I learned, was the culprit behind all my bad moods, all the times I felt too lazy to rise in the morning, all the times I failed to get to the synagogue on time for morning, afternoon, and evening prayers. The *yetzer ha-ra* was the guy who kept distracting me during class with thoughts of female ribs, of how it would feel to sneak up on Feigel Yontiff from behind and hold her in such a way that I could feel her ribs. She was ten and I was eleven. We played a lot. So, the *yetzer ha-ra* advised me: "Get her to play 'The Mummy' or 'Franken-stein' with you. Then sneak up on her like on TV and grab her from behind and squeeze her until you feel her ri ..."

"Gershon!"

"Yes, *ribbe* ... uh ... rebbe."

"Where are we holding?"

"Feigel ... uh ..."

"In the *text!* Where are we up to in the *text?!*—not in your *fantasies.*"

"'And it came to pass that night that the daughters of Lot got their father drunk with wine and ...'"

"No! No no no! We skipped that part! Where are we holding? Have you been day dreaming again?"

"Um ... oh, 'And Avimelech the king of G'rar sent for Sarah the wife of Abraham and he slept with her, and ...'"

"No! Nonononono! We skipped that part, too!"

"'And God opened the womb of Sarah as had been foretold.'"

"Correct! One more time this happens and I will write a note to your parents."

How would I explain to my parents that it wasn't me, that it was the *yetzer ha-ra?* He had managed to sneak into me and was taking over. By the way, I did finally get to feel Feigel's ribs. The "Mummy" idea worked fantastically. She agreed to play the classic fifties movie scene of the helpless female victim, and I instructed my younger brothers and the other kids on the block to hold off on looking for me ("the Mummy") until they heard Feigel scream. Then I instructed Feigel not to scream for at least two minutes. She enjoyed the embrace and suspended screaming for more like five minutes. By then, her ribs were losing their novelty and I was pining for something more and I didn't know what. It would take me another five or six years to figure it out. Not that the Evil Inclination was a poor master. I was a poor disciple.

By thirteen, I started experiencing *hard-ons*, ancient Hebrew for "erections." It took me a while to make the connection between the sensation in my groin and the concept of sex. I had no idea how babies got made. There was no way that you could convince me even at fifteen that my holy, saintly, venerable *rosh yeshiva*, the rabbi who headed my yeshiva, actually merged physically with his wife in that way. You know what I mean. It was inconceivable. How they were able to have kids amazed me to no end. The possibility of immaculate conception did cross my mind on several occasions, and this was years before I'd sneaked a peek at a book about Christianity.

But by thirteen, Feigel and I stopped playing together. We'd say hi to each other in passing, now and then, each of us left with a half-assed smile of naiveté about why it was we weren't playing "The Mummy" anymore. Why it was we weren't playing altogether. I was thirteen, she twelve. Both of us had undergone a major life transition, a transformative rite-of-passage called *Bat Mitzvah* for her, *Bar Mitzvah* for me.

As an Orthodox Jewish boy, Hebrew was a second language to me. Chanting the Torah was second nature. Vowels were superfluous. I needed no Bar-Mitzvah training at all like the hapless *schmeggegs* that are reared in so-called progressive temples and synagogues. And afterwards I was included as part of a *minyan*, which in Orthodox tradition is a quorum of minimally ten males required for collective prayer. Suddenly I was a big shot. If they needed a *minyan*, they could count on me, as little as I was, in spite of my squeaky yet childish voice, and my fantasies notwithstanding.

And girls were out. Just when I started getting interested in girls and in venturing beyond ribs, girls became taboo. From now on it was no touching until after marriage, and then only your wife and only when she wasn't menstruating. That was a scary one for me. What if my strange girl-associated urges continued to grow? How would I deal with so much as four or five years without playing "the Mummy" with someone like Feigel? It got so bad that I would frequent the anatomy section of the local library just so I could get a glimpse of female ribs every now and then.

The Evil Inclination at this point had gone from a tempter to a pain-in-the-ass. It's one thing to play with my mind and talk me into things that felt good. It's another thing to now leave me dangling helplessly with no outlet for my fantasies. Smiling mischievously, the *yetzer ha-ra* walked leisurely off into the sunset, abandoning me with ideas whose expression was now suddenly forbidden.

The subject of the *yetzer ha-ra* now became not only my preoccupation but also the preoccupation of all my teachers at the high-school yeshiva I attended in St. Louis, Missouri.

The Evil One

What was a New York yeshiva boy doing in St. Louis?

Well, I was not happy in New York, and actually dreamed of one day running cattle in Wyoming or growing alfalfa in Poughkeepsie. During Talmud classes in eighth grade I'd drift off into dreamland and doodle along the margins of the sacred writ, as I mentioned before. Don't judge me. Doodling on the margins of talmudic folios was not my invention. A thousand years before, the great commentator *Rashi* (Rabbi Shlomo Yitzchaki) had done the same thing, as had his daughters and sons-in-law, who were known as the *Tosefot*. The only difference was that the doodling of these medieval masters comprised their commentaries and clarification of the virtually cryptic talmudic text, whereas *my* doodling comprised dozens of tiny dots intended as an aerial view of the herd of cows I would one day own.

To this day, I haven't a clue as to why I became so fascinated with the wild west, and with one day becoming a cowboy, or maybe even an Indian. No clue. According to *Rashi* it had to do with my watching too many westerns, especially Hopalong Cassidy. The *Tosefot* disagree, arguing that watching too many westerns may perhaps have been a *result* rather than a cause. In other words, why was I so drawn to westerns to begin with? Other commentators like the thirteenth-century Rabbi Moshe ibn Nachmon of Spain held that my attraction to the ways and means of the wild west had nothing to do with watching TV. After all, he argued, we were only permitted a half an hour of TV a day, and I'd always chosen Zorro who was neither a cowboy *nor* an Indian. The sixteenth-century mystic Rabbi Judah Loew of Prague writes somewhere in his classic *Netivot Olam* that my disdain for living in New York City was what drove me to my fantasies about the wild west.

Whatever the reason, I was soon on a bus to St. Louis where a brand new yeshiva had just been opened by some rabbis from the great yeshiva of Lakewood, New Jersey. Yeshivot, it turns out, were starting to franchise themselves, not for money—at which yeshivot have historically been dismal failures—but for the sake of spreading Torah knowledge and practice across the length and breadth of

America, especially in regions with smaller Jewish communities. So in a way, I was a pioneer, a seasoned New York yeshiva boy shipped off to the wilds of St. Louis, Missouri, for the purpose of strengthening the Jewish community there and serving as reinforcement for the skeletal system of Jewish education that was in its fledgling stages there.

Of course, St. Louis was then and still is a major Jewish community and already had its system of Jewish education well in hand, but it was *modern* Orthodox as opposed to the true and only authentic way, the *ultra*-Orthodox yeshivish way. *We* would show them.

And so I sat there on the bus looking out the window at the passing countryside of New Jersey. Any moment now, I thought, we would be crossing into Pennsylvania, where the landscape would be peppered with men in coonskin caps and long muskets schlepping beaver furs on their shoulders.

Nothing.

Just more cities and towns, more cars and trucks. Ohio was no different. And get this: I didn't see a single solitary Indian in all of Indiana! Illinois was completely void of tall bearded men in top hats splitting wood in front of their log homes. But I didn't give up hope. After all, we hadn't crossed the Mississippi River yet, the final frontier across which the wild west continued to thrive as it had from the very beginning of television.

St. Louis was a real disappointment. Just another metropolis. Desperate, my visions shattered, I withdrew myself into an alternate identity. In no time, I changed my accent and started sounding like Wyatt Earp. I went to a local Salvation Army store and bought a pair of Levis, some used cowboy boots, and a wide belt with a humongous silver buckle engraved with the head of a longhorn. It was an outright shame, I thought, an insult to the wild west, that no one was walking around like this anymore. If I couldn't have the wild west, I was going to become it. Certainly not during my yeshiva schedule, but certainly during the Sabbath when I would sneak away from the yeshiva and walk four miles to the hub of the Jewish community so I could attend synagogue services there. Not that the yeshiva lacked services, but they did lack girls.

Oh my God. What were girls doing on my holy talmudic mind?

Without realizing it, the *yetzer ha-ra* had snuck up behind me even while I was immersed in Torah study and prayer at the yeshiva. I'd become completely distracted figuring out how to win the west when actually the *yetzer ha-ra* had been busily working at other plans that had nothing to do with Clint Eastwood: Girls. I was fifteen, an adolescent, way past puberty, several years without feeling ribs other than my own, preoccupied with the study of how to avert the *yetzer ha-ra*—and now this! The yeshiva had just gone through all the trouble of relocating way way way to the other side of town so that we adolescent yeshiva boys wouldn't get distracted by girls, and here I was walking four long miles back to access the company or proximity of those very girls.

I was ready, too. My hair all brill-creamed and shiny and parted down the middle, a white shirt with a black vest, cowboy boots, shiny silver buckle with the Golden Calf engraved on it, and lots of deodorant since I abhorred showers. The get-up, I realize in retrospect, had little or nothing to do with memorializing the west that no longer was. It had to do with girls. I was dressed to kill, equipped to draw the attention of every female of the opposite gender. To my astonishment, however, I ended up drawing the attention of *everyone*, men, women, children, girls, boys. They'd never seen anything like it. Either I got mistaken for a Jewish member of the Addam's Family, or for the ghost of Jesse James as a teenager.

Following services, some of the fathers of some of the girls approached me bent on satisfying their curiosity. Like, who the hell was this strangely dressed character gracing the synagogue with his vivid presence, not to mention aroma. One after another they approached me, inviting me home for the Sabbath meal, Saturday after Saturday, each time a different family, sometimes a different synagogue, always the same get-up, the only one of its kind I owned. My intention was to be known as a yeshiva boy who stemmed from anywhere but the east coast. My intention was to impress the daughters so they would fall in love with me, revere me, worship me, and maybe even touch the lapel of my shirt. As a New Yorker, I would fail. As an Orthodox Jewish cow hand, I would be such an anomaly that no one could resist. And I was right.

"So where are you from?"

"Um ... Dodge City."

"Dodge City? Are you here visiting relatives?"

"Nope. Goin' to the yeshiva o'er yonder."

"Wow. I didn't know there were any Jews in Dodge City. What does your father do there?"

"Owns a ranch."

"Wow. A Jewish cowboy. Amazing. Do you have a herd ... oh, wait, Diane come here and meet this ... uh ... this is my daughter Diane, and you are ...?"

"Gersh ... uh ... Hank. Hank Winkler. Pleased to make your acquaintance, ma'am."

"Harry! Harry, come here. I want you to meet this young man. He goes to the yeshiva and he's from Dodge City. His father owns a ..."

"Yeah, we met. He was over at our place last *Shabbat*. But I thought he was from Oklahoma. Aren't you from Bird Creek, Oklahoma ...?"

"Hey, *gut shabbos*, how's it going? I see you two have met Gus Kedidlehopper from Montana. His father owns a ra ..."

"Gus? I thought his name was Hank ...?

"Montana? I thought he was from Dodge City ...?"

Needless to say, my ruse didn't last too long. So I decided to retire into exile on the isolated campus of the yeshiva where I buried myself deeper and deeper into the truths of Torah, perfected my character, and shifted my untreated horninesss from thoughts of girls to thoughts of boys, often getting turned on while wrestling with my dorm mates in our pajamas until Shlomo the dorm counselor would walk in to chastise us for not going to sleep. But it was all innocent. Just your normal unspoken adolescent male homotendencitis at work.

The Evil One

The sons of Israel are not suspected of homosexual behavior.
Therefore it is permitted for them
to sleep together in the same bed,
but not regularly.

⋖§ 16th century Rabbi Yosef Karo:
Shulchan Aruch, Ev'n Ha-Ezer 24:1

And so I threw myself lock, stock'n'barrel at the mercy of the
Torah, the spiritual regimen of study, practice, and self-discipline
that had preserved my people for 3,500 years. I don't want to brag,
or anything. But by the time I turned seventeen I was the holiest
man on the planet. So holy, that even the miserly three hours a day
of secular high school curriculum felt to me an impediment to my
spiritual evolution and service to God. Suddenly the yeshiva in St.
Louis wasn't spiritual enough, pure enough; it was too secular for
me. I wanted to immerse myself in God and Torah all day and night,
not a mere eight hours a day. I needed to drop out of high school and
go to the Holy Land, to Israel, for only there would I discover authentic religious devotion and pure yeshiva learning.

So I quit yeshiva high school in the middle of the third year and
went to Jerusalem to study in a real-time, old-time yeshiva where I
grew into a holy man, steeped night and day in learning, prayer,
psalmic meditation, biblical contemplation, talmudic confrontation,
and herring. I also took up *mussar*, the study of ancient and medieval
writings about how to be a *mensch*, a good person, a pleasant person, a person of faith and humility, ever-evolving my character
through self-examination and introspection until I acquired traits of
religious devotion and piety that even made God gag.

Says the Holy Blessed One:
"I have created the *yetzer ha-ra*,
and I have also created Torah
as its antidote."

⋖§ Babylonian Talmud, Kidushin 30b

Indeed, I was now completely immune. I hadn't seen or heard from the Evil Inclination since I stopped using Brillcream and walking four miles to see girls. I was free of it forever. The antidote had worked. Once in Jerusalem, my life was filled to the brim with nothing but Torah.

> Anyone who proclaims
> "I have nothing but Torah!"
> has indeed nothing,
> not even Torah.
>
> **⋙ Babylonian Talmud, *Yevamot* 109b**

In fact, I found myself in absolute ecstasy. I had become so spiritual and religious that it was actually blissful to do without material comfort, to get up for prayer at seven in the morning during a chilly Jerusalem winter in a flophouse yeshiva that so lacked funds it couldn't afford plaster to cover its holy walls or a plumber to repair its single leaky shower. (Not that the leak was the problem; on the contrary, it was thanks to the leak that we were able to shower to begin with since the *faucet* didn't work.) Each morning at this destitute old rubble of a *yeshiva* I would awaken to the sweet, croaky chanting of the seventy-seven year old rabbi who ran the place, as he shuffled slowly through the frozen corridors of the dorm, limping on the leg that had been shot clear through during the Israeli War of Independence in 1948 while he was deeply immersed in talmudic study and while my mother was pregnant with me.

"Kum l'avodat ha-borey" he would chant, decked in his prayer shawl and phylacteries, and knocking gently on every door. Translation: "Arise to the service of the Creator." What a beautiful way to start your day, serving God in prayer and meditation, study and introspection, including a thirty minute discourse on the hazards of succumbing to that sneaky sonofabitch, the *yetzer ha-ra*. Breakfast was then made available to us—a necessity for the life of the physical

vehicle of the soul—predictably old bread donated to us by a more affluent "American" yeshiva down the street, some mildewed strawberry jelly, hot water with an assortment of well-worn tea bags, and some salad concocted from vegetables grown on Saturn.

Following breakfast we would head straight for the *beis medrash*, or study hall, literally "house of interpretation," where we would pore for hours over the sacred, gigantic volumes of the Talmud, the compilation of some seven centuries of rabbinic wit, lore, ethics, scriptural interpretation, and legalistic discussion, spanning from around 200 B.C.E.F.G. to around 500 A.C.D.C.. The beautiful thing about all this, is that nobody had sent us here. We had come on our own volition to serve the Creator with no ulterior motive. And although there were some disciples who looked forward to acquiring real estate in the World To Come as a reward for their religious devotion in the here-and-now, I was certainly not one of them since my family always rented.

Delicately balanced alongside our Talmuds were piles of books containing medieval as well as latter-day rabbinic commentaries on the Talmud, plus more volumes of further commentaries explaining the other commentaries, *ad infinitum*. And so we would sit or stand or walk or sway for hours and hours while studying, absorbing, disputing, assessing and discussing, totally oblivious to the "outside world," totally unconscious of the material realm. The world was falling apart, Israel was at war with a half dozen Arab armies, New Yorkers were getting mugged in Central Park, American soldiers were getting blown up in Vietnam, East Germans were getting mowed down at the Berlin Wall—and here we were studying about who was liable if a person carrying a barrel plows into a person carrying a beam, or what it was that our ancestors sang as they danced toward the sacred House of the Water Spring during the autumn celebrations.

But this was not about indifference, or sticking our heads in the sand. It was about clinging to reality in a world gone mad. What was going on out there was stupid, idiotic, unnecessary, foolish, distorted expressions of masculinity. In the yeshiva, however, our masculinity was defined not by aggression and violence, or by possessiveness and vengeance. Rather, it was defined by mastery over the Evil Inclination, the culprit behind all that chaos in the "outside world." As for us undernourished yeshiva boys, we were simply behaving in relation to what the world *ought* to be like out there, not to what it had become as a result of what people were doing in it.

> What if a person planted stolen tomato seeds? Will they
> not sprout, since they were stolen? Or what if a man has
> an affair with another man's wife? Will she not become
> pregnant, since it was a forbidden union? On the
> contrary! For the world goes on as it is accustomed to,
> and the fools who abuse it will reap their consequences,
> while the righteous will reap their rewards.
>
> **Babylonian Talmud, *Avodah Zarah* 54b**

The Talmud records that days before the fall of Jerusalem some ninteteen hundred years ago, the Roman legion commander, Vespasianus, invited the venerable Rabbi Yochanan ben Zakkai to ask for anything and it would be granted to him. Did he plead for the Temple to be spared? Did he plead for the lifting of the siege around Jerusalem? Did he plead for a new mall? Nope. He said: "Give me Yavneh and its sages and leave us to study our Torah" (Babylonian Talmud, *Avot D'Rebbe Nattan* 4:6). Life ought to be peaceful, meditative, introspective, transformative, loving, spiritual. Let the world go about its helter-skelter spin of self-destruction. We yeshiva boys, on the other hand, in the tradition of our ancestors, were going to stay cool and study. We, on the other hand, were not going to succumb to the foolishness that afflicts people because they are too weak to stand up to the *yetzer ha-ra*. No. We were going to remain steadfast in the contemplation of the Will of God as interpreted for us by our prophets of old and by our sages of yore. We were going to bathe ourselves in what was Truth and Rightness, and in what was divine and holy.

God was I horny.

The Evil One

He who is greater than his fellow,
his Evil Inclination is also
that much greater.

⋖ **Babylonian Talmud, *Sukab* 52a**

I couldn't take it any more. I was eighteen and burning. The Evil Inclination was sneaking in the back door and was sabotaging my saintliness with lewd thoughts and sensations. The holier I was becoming the hornier I got. I would barely recite a scriptural or talmudic passage when somehow it would acquire sexual connotations of one sort or another. We'd be studying about how a man needed to separate from his wife during her period and I would get this image of what it might have been like for the guy *before* he had to separate or when they got back together *after* her period. Like what were they doing? How did it feel for a man being inside a woman?

Oh my God, it was time to rise for the afternoon prayer and I had a hard on.

There was only one legitimate way out: I had to get married and I had to get married quick. But the Evil Inclination had other plans.

For thus is the skill of the Evil Inclination,
that first he tells you to do such and such
good deed, and on the morrow he tells you
to just do this and that innocent thing,
until eventually he will have you worshiping idols.

⋖ **Babylonian Talmud, *Shabbat* 105b**

Meals on Wheels was invented by the Evil Inclination in the guise of organized outreach to the homebound destitute and elderly. In Jerusalem, in the Spring of 1967, it attracted amongst its volunteers an incredibly sexy Yemenite Jewish woman who was married with children.

And me.

My elderly *Rosh Yeshiva* was against my participating. I remember his words exactly:

"Ay, Gershen, Gershen, Gershen. Zeh ha-yetzer ha-ra sh'mazmin ot'cha l'kach. Tish'ma eylie v'tisha'er poh b'beit ha-medrash v'ta'asok ba-torah, v'acherim ya'asu et ha-chessed ha-zot."

Translation: "Ah, Gershon, Gershon, Gershon. It is the Evil Inclination who is inviting you. Listen to me and remain here in the House of Study and immerse yourself in Torah, and let others perform this charitable act."

"But *rebbe*, I feel that doing this work would be putting my Torah studies into action."

"Ay, Gershen, Gershen, Gershen. It is the Evil Inclination who speaks thus. Wisely did our sages teach that one should not interrupt one's study of Torah even for deeds of charity, unless there is no one else taking care of it. But if others are tending to it, there is no excuse for you to interrupt your studies (Jerusalem Talmud, *P'sachim* 3:7 [24a])."

"But it feels so strong to me, *rebbe*, the need to finally just go out there and actually *do* the teachings of the Torah."

"Ay, Gershen, Gershen, Gershen. The Evil One is very clever. He knows how to talk us into anything. He uses ruses that sound so pure and innocent but which ultimately become our downfall. You are young yet. You will have plenty of time to perform acts of benevolence in the world, but now is your time for absorbing, for studying. You are not needed right now to do the work, only to do the learning and growing."

"But I feel that doing the work will help me to grow, to integrate my learning."

"Ay, Gershen, Gershen, Gershen."

He argued no further, that sweet old man, only stood there on his bullet-ridden leg smiling that wise, knowing smile. He knew that I couldn't be talked out of it. It was too late. The Evil One had already gotten me by the balls. I had travelled across thousands of miles of oceans and seas to study Torah, and here I was looking to save the world.

> Rabbi Avahu of Caesaria (3rd century) sent his son to study Torah in Tiberias. Later he was told that his son was preoccupied with tending to the dead. He wrote to his son, saying: "Was there a lack of cemeteries in Caesaria that I had to send you all the way to Tiberias to tend to the dead?"
>
> **◆§ Jerusalem Talmud, P'sachim 3:7 [24a]**

"Ay, Gershen, Gershen, Gershen" would haunt me the rest of my life whenever I would surrender to the Evil Inclination. I would then smile back sheepishly at the image of the old man with the white scraggly beard swaying back and forth in front of his pile of books balanced perfectly atop a splintering *shtender*, or wooden book stand.

I signed up for Friday duty with Meals on Wheels and fought hard not to fantasize so much as touching the sleeve of the very attractive Yemenite woman who handed me meals from the van and pointed out the shacks to which I was to deliver them. I thought of her. I dreamed of her. She was married. I was committing mental adultery. The Evil One had won. He was destroying everything I had striven so hard and long to achieve in my soul. My saintliness was being drained from me ounce by ounce. I was losing blood. I wanted that woman. I used to look forward to Friday because it meant that the Holy Sabbath was approaching. Now I was looking forward to Friday because it meant that the Yemenite woman was approaching.

> One who gazes lustfully at so much as the small finger of a married woman— it is as if he commits adultery with her.
>
> **◆§ Babylonian Talmud, Kalah, Ch. 1**

I needed to get married. It was the only way out. The woman was not Orthodox and therefore much more prone to having an affair than I was. There was still hope for me. I was after all a seasoned warrior in the ever-continuing battle with the Evil Inclination. I had the strength to withstand him under any circumstance. It was up to me. She stood no chance. She hadn't made any advances yet, true, but it was only a matter of time. She smiled at me that funny kind of smile.

Of course the truth is that it was all in my confused head. As far as she was concerned, I was nothing more than a skinny eunuch with a yarmulka. God was I horny. I really really needed to get married to someone. Anyone. I knew damn well what the Evil One wanted from me. He wanted me to have an affair with a married woman or to at least entertain forbidden thoughts about it. Or he wanted me to engage in premarital sex—a major no-no, I was taught, although nowhere in the Torah does it state that you have to be married to have sex. Or he wanted me to spill my seed masturbating—an even more serious prohibition, I'd been taught. But I wasn't going to cave in. He had to try harder than Meals on Wheels. In fact, I simply quit. There. No more Evil Inclination.

Or so I thought.

One Friday as I was returning from another yeshiva with some old bread, I noticed a blind man awkwardly making his way across a busy intersection. I approached him and asked him if he needed an escort. He accepted. I walked him to his apartment, a one-room suite in a decrepit old hotel. It turned out he was a recluse living off some pension, in dire need of companionship, someone to talk to now and then. So I volunteered, not knowing he was the Evil Inclination disguised as a blind lonely man. Our discussions began innocently enough with philosophy. He was an admitted atheist, and this only gave me a further sense of divine purpose: to try and bring him to the belief in God.

"Ay, Gershen, Gershen, Gershen," I heard the warning chant of my *rebbe*. But it was too late. In the midst of our third visit together, he silenced my theological ranting and pointed to the ceiling. From above came the sounds of a violently creaking bed and some heavy-duty moaning and groaning in the voices of a woman and a man.

"Prostitute," he said, smiling. He reached for his crotch and began to caress himself through his trousers. "She comes down to my room sometimes," he went on. "Would you like to try her?"

I fled the hotel and never again saw the blind man. Behind me, the Evil Inclination roared with laughter. "I was only kidding!" I heard him shout to me, but I was not amused. It had gone far enough. There was nothing left for me to do in my war against the Evil One than to get married so that sex would no longer be on my mind.

The Evil Inclination, cognizant of my plan, immediately got to work. No less than two weeks later he hired a new cook for the yeshiva, a recent immigrant from Morocco. She was often accompanied by her daughter, the most beautiful, most exotic woman I had ever laid my eyes on—by accident, of course, lest you think in your lewd minds that I actually went out of my way to gaze upon her.

Day and night I lusted after her, dreamed about her, fantasized about her, envisioned life with her. In the study hall, the vast pages of the Talmud before me transformed into a scenario of vast desert lands, the words became distant images of me riding into the blazing south wind on a feisty camel, with one arm wrapped around my beloved and the other around a volume of Maimonides' Code of Jewish Law. Together we rode off into the horizon of Talmudic commentaries who graced the margins of the text, in search of an oasis in which to set up our tent and make passionate love until the rains came, our goats nibbling rhythmically at the fringes of my sand-speckled prayer shawl.

I wanted this woman bad. She was single, her family religious, and even returned my lovesick stares whenever I would swoon in her presence as I staggered into the kitchen for second, third, and fourth helpings of soggy salad.

I went to the *Rosh Yeshivah*.

"I feel I am ready to get married."

"Ay, Gershen, Gershen, Gershen, ayayayayay. The Evil One is at it again."

"On the contrary, Rebbe, this is the one sure way to get rid of him once and for all so that I could just concentrate on study and prayer."

"Ay, Gershen, Gershen, Gershen, ayayayayay. You are only giving in to him when you should be training yourself to avoid his antics."

"Rebbe, I really want to be married. I have someone in mind."

"Yes? Who?"

"I don't know her name."

"Ay, Gershen, Gershen, Gershen, you don't even know her name. See how desperate he has made you? Remember what God said: 'I created the Evil Inclination, and I created Torah as the antidote' (Babylonian Talmud, *Kidushin* 30b). Return to your studies. I want so much to ordain you, you are rabbi material. But you need to stay put and concentrate on your studies."

"I don't want to be a rabbi. I want to get married. I love this woman."

"You don't even know her name. How could you love her already?"

"She's the cook's daughter."

"The cook's daughter?"

"Yes."

"Ay, Gershen, Gershen, Gershen, ayayayayay. Her name is Ayelet and she belongs to a whole different culture than what you are used to. It is no match. Leave it be. Go back to your studies."

"I love her. She is the one. I know it in my heart and guts. I can adjust to her cultural ways, and she to mine. Can you please set up a meeting between us? This is so important to me, Rebbe. Please."

"Ay, Gershen, Gershen, Gershen. What's going to be from you?"

Within three days I was approached by Feivel, a perpetual American bachelor who made a career out of living in dorms and studying in *yeshivot* around the world. He had a message for me from the *Rosh Yeshivah:* I was to be at the cook's house tomorrow night at eight. He then handed me a slip of paper with the cook's address, and looked at me funny.

"Are you sure you want to do this?"

"I've never been more sure of anything in my entire life, Feivel."

"You haven't lived that long yet."

"With this woman I will live long enough to confirm my decision."

"Do you want me to come with you?"

"No, thank you, Feivel. I can do this alone."

"I hope you know what you're getting yourself into."

"Don't worry. I'll be fine."

"The *Rosh Yeshivah* didn't seem too happy about this."

"I know. He'll be happy at the wedding celebration. I'll show him how much he underestimated me."

The next night I applied my deodorant and walked down the severely cracked pavement of the steeply sloping street that led to the Bucharian sector of Jerusalem where many Oriental and North African Jewish families lived. I stepped off the paved road onto a dirt side road and started looking for the cook's address. This was going to be so exciting. I was actually going to live out my dream of romancing this incredibly beautiful Moroccan Goddess. Together we would stroll leisurely down the narrow, winding streets of antiquity toward the Falafel place, have a bite to eat, discuss our dreams, fall in love—wow. There *is* a God.

The cook opened the door, smiled at me, and led me into a smoke-filled room with wall to wall uncles. The patriarchs studied me as I was given a seat at the head of a long table and offered me chick peas and strong whiskey, an Arabic kind of whiskey known as Arak.

I ate and drank amid the garroulous conversations between the uncles, waiting eagerly for my beloved to be ushered into my presence. But there was no sign of her. Perhaps she was in her room preparing herself for me in her deep deep desire to please me and win me over. In the meantime the patriarchs began to drill me: What did my father do for a living? What kind of skills did I have? How

long had I been studying at the yeshiva? How many siblings did I
have? Did my family own land in America? Goats? Mules? Horses?
How was I intending to support Ayelet? Did I plan to return to the
United States? Would I be living in Israel? Here, have some more
chick peas. Here, have another glass of Arak. When did I envision the
wedding taking place? How soon could my parents make the journey to meet them? Could my siblings come, too?

From the corner of my eye I noticed the door to an adjoining
room slightly ajar—just enough for my beloved fantasy to peek with
one eye into the smoke-filled living room to observe her betrothed
being interrogated by the patriarchs of her clan. The smoke rose to
the ceiling and formed the image of my *Rosh Yeshivah*. The tumult
of the half Arabic, half Hebraic conversations of the uncles turned
into the chant of my sweet elder master as his image floated toward
me: "Ay, Gershen, Gershen, Gershen, ayayayayayayay!"

The old man was right. My God! I hadn't even dated the woman
and already I was being married off, and not to her, mind you, but
to a clan of uncles! I asked to be excused, and staggered out of the
house amid roaring patriarchic laughter, fleeing into the dark
Jerusalem streets.

It was back to Torah for me. No more works of benevolence, and
no more fantasies of getting married. The *Rosh Yeshivah* was right.
I belonged in the writ, not the deed. I was still too naive, too innocent, too trusting. The world outside the yeshiva was fraught with
obstacles, replete with stumbling blocks. I belonged in the safety of
the yeshiva walls, immersed day and night in study, prayer, character development, and mildewed jam.

And there I indeed remained, safe from the clutches of the Evil
Inclination as the Six Day War erupted, raged, and climaxed in time
for the Holy Sabbath.

Chapter Three

The Color Olive

As far as you think you've fled from me,
is as near as you've actually come toward me.
The more you avoid me, the more
you empower me. The harder you strive to
counteract me, the more miserable
your life will become.

✍ The Evil Inclination

Once upon a time, I stood in front of a very wide wall mirror and saw this skinny, pale, bald-shaven man-boy looking me right in the eye. He looked awful familiar but I couldn't quite place him at that particular time. Across one chest pocket a name tag was sewn, and it read "Winkler," and across the other chest pocket the words "U.S. Army." I stood there for a long time, trying to reconcile the paradox, the contradiction, of these two so very contrasting concepts: Winkler and U.S. Army.

Only a few weeks earlier I had been immersed in yeshiva studies in the heart of Jerusalem, and now I was standing in a giant bathroom in Fort Jackson, South Carolina, because I needed to get married to counter the Evil Inclination, and I had decided to return to the states to find a wife, and they were drafting people for this war in Vietnam, and I didn't want to get married and then get torn from my family by the draft, and I didn't want to dodge the draft, either. So I'd enlisted to get it over with so I could get married and start a family and maybe even have sex.

As I pondered the dreadful realization that I was actually in the army, I unbuttoned my olive green fly and pee'd into what appeared to me to be a gigantic communal urinal but which I later discovered was the communal wash basin. The urinals were at the other end of the latrine. I finished peeing and turned on the faucet, wondering why the government couldn't afford regular flush urinals.

While I stood there growing increasingly pale with increasing awareness of my not being home in Brooklyn; of my having been sentenced to three years of servitude to the government of the United States—a thunderous roar startled me back to the more immediately relevant fact that I was in essence a particle of feces. The revelation emanated from a stocky, broad-shouldered drill-corporal whose breath penetrated my neck and shoulders like a potent dose of eucalyptic vapor. His booming voice echoed through the hollows of my bones and in between my red and white blood corpuscles, sending amino acids helter-skelter up and down my shakras. He continued screaming at the top of what was probably at one time his lungs and had over the years evolved into a kazoo. What he screamed was totally unintelligible, but it resonated deep enough inside of my being for me to understand that he was unhappy with my loitering in the bathroom contemplating my poor excuse for a reflection. Not wanting to start my three-year sentence on the wrong foot, I moved rapidly out of the latrine and into the barracks area to join my comrades who were by then clad in sparkling olive T-shirts and shorts and sandwiched snugly betwixt coarse olive blankets and starched olive sheets.

But the drill corporal was still foaming at the mouth and followed me to my bunk.

"Duffus!" he shouted at the nape of my neck as I struggled to unbuckle the brass government-issue buckle of my olive drab green belt. I went to yeshiva all my life and had no idea that Duffus was not someone's name and that the drill corporal was therefore not addressing the guy in the lower bunk. So I continued my struggle with the buckle. When I realized I was getting nowhere with it I decided to work on unbuttoning my shirt.

"Dick head!" he shouted. And I felt so relieved he wasn't after me anymore and was instead picking on two other comrades-in-arms: Duffus and Dickhead. Boy, I mused, trying to separate some loose olive green thread from one of the olive green buttons, I thought *Jewish* names were funny. Non-Jewish names were even stranger.

"Butt face!" he bellowed, his pitch sounding higher and higher. God was he angry, and I was so relieved he wasn't yelling at me. His shouting alone was traumatic enough for a yeshiva boy like me who had been taught to always communicate with humbleness and in a soft tone of voice. My father, too, always spoke in a very low voice, so low that I often had to shuffle real close to his mouth to make out what it was he was saying. Needless to say, we were always very close.

"Goddammit!!" he screamed, and so loud I could have sworn I saw his tonsils fly across the room. Or perhaps it was some leftover food particles that had gotten free of the narrow spaces between his teeth. Screaming at me, it turned out, was his way of flossing. I started wondering why he had to stand right behind me while screaming at Duffus, Dickhead, Buttface, and Goddammit. And what kind of names were they? I was used to Moishe, Yankel, Dovid'l and Yitz.

A powerful shock vibrated through my spinal chord, bouncing up and about from shakra to shakra and sending desperate messages to my brain pleading that I turn around and respond to the *meschuggeneh* who was trying so hard to get my attention with the knuckles of his right hand pressed against my cerebellum. I turned to face him, my fingers still fumbling with the shirt buttons. And as I swung around to face him, I knocked an ash can clear off one of the columns, spilling soddy water and soggy cigarette butts all over the freshly waxed barracks floor.

"Yes?" I asked, wondering whether I needed to address him as Sir or Highness, and what it was that I had knocked onto the floor and why it was hanging from the post in front of my bunk to begin with ... that is, according to *Rashi*, a foremost medieval commentator on the Talmud.

"Yes WHAT?!" he screamed. By now my ears were ringing with a hum that has lasted to this day, and has become so loud even others are hearing it and are attributing it to clandestine government experiments.

"Yes what WHAT?" I replied, inquiring what the *yes-what* was about.

"Yes what what WHAT?!!" he cried, the pitch of his voice so high it was barely audible. I heard several dogs barking in the distance and the nearby sound of glass shattering.

"Yes what what what WHAT?" I asked. After all, I was accustomed to questions, and to questions about questions from my years of talmudic studies and the pilpulic intellectual gymnastics they involved.

"It's *Yes, Drill Corporal,* meat head!!" he shouted. "I want you to re-wax this whole floor and buff it. Get it?"

"Well, wax I understand. I always helped my mother wax the floor for *shabbos.* But what's a buff?"

"See that machine over in the corner?"

I looked. It was a big, heavy looking machine and I didn't want anything to do with it because I couldn't for the life of me identify it as anything remotely associated with anything with which I have ever been remotely associated.

"I see it, but what is it?"

"That's a buffer, ass-hole."

"A bufferasshole? And how do you use it?"

"You're such a wise guy, you'll figure it out."

"So can I maybe do all this in the morning? It's pretty late, you know, I'm pooped. Moreover, I haven't had a chance to recite my evening prayers yet. By the way, do they serve kosher food here?" I looked around at my comrades only to find most of them ducking beneath their olive blankets. At the time it seemed to me that their concealment was an attempt to get some sleep with the lights still on. But in retrospect I realize it was not very different from when they would scurry for cover in later weeks when it was my turn at grenade practice.

Sure enough, the human bomb detonated and the noise was so loud I couldn't make out the words blaring forth from what was once the drill corporal but had now been transformed into an animated Picasso piece that had broken loose from its canvas. When he completed his single-breath'd repertoire, he walked off to the latrine to wash up for bed, and left me with the distinct impression that he would remember me in the morning, as well as through*out* my basic training period. It got clear to me that I might have irritated him. And it got me thinking that perhaps there was some way I could make it up to him. We could become friends. Maybe I could even circumcise him some day. These thoughts flooded my mind as I crawled about on my knees and rubbed fresh wax across the floor amid numerous complaints from the audience.

I tried waxing as fast as I could, skimping a little here and skipping a little there. Then I went to the buffer machine, plugged it in and pressed the only lever I could find. The machine took off with a *gevalt,* sending me flailing in all directions across the floor as I hung on for dear life to both the handle and lever.

"Let go, motherfucker!!" someone yelled from a nearby top bunk. I released my grip and the machine took off without me, sending me flying across the slippery wax floor and underneath one of the bunkbeds. The buffer machine sped across the barracks and slammed hard into one of the columns sending yet another ash can to the floor, spilling filthy water and cigarette butts all over the fresh wax. The corporal was now in the doorway of the latrine, brushing his teeth and gripping a white government-issue towel. He cussed beneath his breath and through his toothpaste, some of it dripping onto the floor. "When you're done re-waxing the floor again, bean-brain, I want you to clean out the wash basin in here!" he yelled. "It smells like *piss!*" And he left the room.

So I spent my first night in the army waxing and buffing and cleaning the latrine. By the time they blew taps I was the most well-known soldier in Company B, whose marching chant I could never for the life of me figure out: "B! B! Beat your meat!"

I climbed up to the top bunk that was assigned to me, slid underneath the tightly-tucked white sheet and olive blanket, shut my eyes, and went to sleep in no time at all. Waiting at the doorway to my dreams was my teacher, the elder *Rosh Yeshiva*, shaking his head from side to side with that "when will you ever learn" sort of smile.

———————

"Ay, Gershen, Gershen, Gershen, so is this better? Is this better than learning Torah in the yeshiva?"

"Of course not, rebbe, nothing in the world is better than learning Torah."

"So why did you leave?"

"I had to, rebbe, I had to get married."

"And there is a shortage of women in Jerusalem?"

"Not at all, only I ... uh ... I ... "

"And I suppose that right now you're at some kind of weekend retreat for singles, then?"

"Oh, this? Nononono, this is the army. United States Army."

"Ayayay, Gershen, Gershen, Gershen."

"No, rebbe, you don't understand ... "

"It's not so important that I understand, but do you understand?"

"Me? Uh ... sure. I ... uh ... I came back here because I decided I really want to live in the states. I'm more at home here. And I wanted to settle down, get married, start a family, start living the Torah, not just studying it."

"Already you've forgotten Meals On Wheels?"

"Oh that. I was a young kid then."

"It was six months ago."

"Yeah, but ... uh ... I ... that was different. I'm more clear now about what I want to do with my life."

"I see. More clear. And that explains, then, why you're about to spend three precious years of your life as a soldier."

"I told you, rebbe, I wanted to get married."

"Yes, yes, of course, forgive me. You joined the army so you could get married and live the Torah."

"Yeah, that's it."

"Tell me, Gershen, how long are your fellow soldiers going to be in the army?"

"Most of them are in for two years, rebbe."

"And you are in for three?"

"Yeah, I joined, so then you serve three when you join, when you volunteer."

"I see, so they who didn't want to join, will serve two years, and you who volunteered, will serve three years."

"I know it doesn't make much sense, but I had to join so I could get married."

"And if you would have been drafted, then you couldn't get married?"

"I could, but they would probably have taken me while I was married and I'd have been separated from my wife and maybe even from my children!"

"Ayyyy, Gershen, Gershen, Gershen, what's going to be of you?"

———————

The rabbi stepped aside and let me pass into the most beautiful, deepest sleep I'd ever experienced. At least he wouldn't be waking me up early in the morning for prayers anymore. I could just sleep and sleep and sleep …

… Aaaaah, the feeling was beautiful. No—ecstatic. It felt tranquil, comfortable. Paradise enveloped my being. It was the kind of feeling I will never be able to explain fully, to describe coherently. The kind of serenity one experiences after having worked out a payment plan with the IRS for back taxes. In fact, I was so deep in that REM place that even the shrilling cries of Master Drill Sergeant Inerderein's master drill whistle never registered with any part of either of my ears. But slowly my consciousness gently aroused my subconsciousness which in turn dipomatically informed my brain to—as Drill Sergeant Inerderein so masterfully put it at the top of his lungs and at the door of my left ear—"Get the hell up, you deaf motherfucker!!"

> One should be diligent to rise in the
> morning with vim and vigor
> like a leopard to do service
> unto the Creator.
>
> ✌ Babylonian Talmud, *Avot* 1:2

Startled, I opened my eyes to a bare white ceiling and realized that I was still where I had been the previous day and that the entire nightmare of being in the army was not the dream I had hoped it would be. Startled by the loud shouting and cussing of several drill sergeants and their wild packs of cadre—and by the thundering roar in my left ear of the word "Now!!"—I slid quickly out of bed and into the abyss of empty space. I had forgotten that I was on the top bunk of a double-decker but was instantly reminded of this when my nose hit my bunkmate's footlocker.

I looked out the window of the barracks as I reached for my trousers with one hand while the other held a white towel pressed firmly against my bloody nose. It was pitch dark and I wondered why they had gotten us up so early. Most problematic, however, was putting on *tefillin* while it was still dark. Morning prayers needed to be said in the morning, not in the middle of the night; at the rise of dawn, not at revelle.

Amid the shouts steaming forth from the bloodshot drill instructors I was able to make out some of the words, and they had to do with chow, mess hall, and shit heads. It occurred to me that maybe there was something in there about breakfast, too. As Master Drill Sergeant Inerderein approached me to investigate the bloody red towel I was holding, I removed it from my nose and asked him about kosher meals. After all, I was serving in the United States Army, set up to defend our constitution, which, in turn, guaranteed freedom of religious practice for all. For all—I was soon to learn—except bewildered, disoriented, bald basic trainees. Master Drill Sergeant Inerderein looked at me with bloodshot eyes, a shade of red spreading rapidly across his square, tight-skinned face, and because he held too much rage than would be worth directing at any one individual, he directed it at the entire platoon of scurrying trainees and shouted: "You studs think you're on some kind of packaged tour, or something! Well I'm telling you right now that this is not a goddam hotel! This is the United States Army! And you damn well better get used to the idea! Now fall out and I don't wanna hear anything from anybody about anything!! Is that clear?!"

"Yes, drill sergeant!" we shouted obediently.

"Louder!"

"YES, DRILL SERGEANT!!"

The drill sergeant then dropped his face into mine, eyeballed me fiercely and said: "The last Jewish guy we had down here who kept kosher decided to give up that stuff rather than get recycled for another couple of months of basic training. And believe me, boy, you don't wanna be in this place any longer than you really have to."

We fell out, which means we stumbled outside to stand in an orderly formation in the pitch dark of the predawn hours, chilled to the bone and scared to the marrow. The flag was hoisted, platoon sergeants shouted "All present and accounted for!" and we were told to stand "at ease." Master Drill Sergeant Inerderein then mounted an elevated platform, looked at us with eyes more piercing than the rising sun, and addressed us:

"I'm Master Drill Sergeant Inerderein and that's how you will address me! Some of you have seen me before, and others—those of you who have not seen me before—are seeing me now! Is that clear?!!"

"YESSIR!!"

"It's Yes, Master Drill Sergeant Inerderein!!"

"YES, MASTER DRILL SERGEANT INERDEREIN!!"

"Your training period will last eight weeks. I know some of you baldies are going to fail the first time around and you'll be recycled into another company to do it over and over and over again until you get it right. We'll treat you fair if you treat us fair and do your best. And another thing! Here in Company B, Second Battalion, Tenth Brigade, everyone is equal! I don't care if you're a damn jew, a nigger, or a polack—you're in the army now and your drawbacks don't count here! Okay! Platoon sergeants! Move 'em out!"

It was perhaps one of the most inspiring and articulate speeches I'd ever heard and it nearly moved me to tears.

After a series of shouting of commands between drill sergeants, we were scurried by a cadre of barking drill corporals and herded into a warm, bacon-stenched mess hall where we were commanded to shout our last names first, first names last, and join the chow line. I quickly drank a glass of orange juice, grabbed a hard boiled egg, and ran back to the barracks to do my morning prayers while everyone was busy with breakfast. Back at the vacated quarters I reached hurriedly into the bottom of my footlocker and withdrew the blue velvet bag that contained my phylacteries. I rolled up my left sleeve and wrapped the black leather straps seven times around my goose-pimpled arm, adjusted the black square leather box which contained the text from the Hebrew scriptures concerning the wearing of the black leather box containing the text of the Hebrew scriptures concerning ... then proceeded to wrap a second black leather box over my forehead above my "third eye," and recited the appropriate Hebraic prayers that accompanied the ritual.

As I left the travails of basic training behind and merged deeper and deeper with the alternate reality of prayerful meditation, the tumult of army life faded into a silence that both mystified me and comforted me. It felt so warm and serene to envelop myself in this ever so familiar state of consciousness, swaying to and fro with increasing fervor as I engaged my creator in deep communion. I was in a state of divine grace, safe and cushioned from the harsh corporeal reality of real corporals and intimidating regimens. Indeed, I felt like I was being watched, truly seen.

And I was.

"What the hell you doin', boy?" a drill voice boomed in, tearing me abruptly from Nirvana, sending angels and cherubim into sudden flight, their feathers raining all over the planet. "You some kind of Buddhist or some shit like that?" I was in the middle of prayer, so I didn't reply and simply continued what must have sounded to him like strange tantric murmurings. "HEY, WINKLER!! I'M TALKING TO YOU, BOY!!"

> It is forbidden to interrupt one's prayers even to
> return the greeting of an Israelite king. But ... if he
> sees snakes or scorpions approaching him and in a
> place where these creatures are known to be deadly,
> he interrupts his prayer and flees.

⤳ Maimonides: *Mishnah Torah, Hil'chot T'filah* 6:9

The sergeant backed off and sat on my footlocker waiting for me to finish. And when I did, he said: "So you're still gonna carry on with this religious stuff? You're never gonna make it outta here with that kind of attitude. I wanna see your ass out in front of the mess hall in fifteen minutes." He got up and walked away. I felt triumphant. They could take from me my dignity, my freedom, my sense of existence, but they couldn't take from me my *tefillin*.

Fifteen minutes later we were herded from the mess hall to the medical building for innoculations, then to the supply building for military issue duffle bags, then to this other place to have our names and serial numbers stenciled onto the duffle bags, then to this other place to receive our military-issue clothing and underwear: Come on, move that line. Where the hell you think you are, Macy's? Let's go, dammit, keep it moving! Next! What's that, boy? You don't like the size of that shirt? Well, I don't like the size of your mouth, now git! Hey, Joe, bring me another box of large trousers—I got another bunch of shorties coming through! Alright, what's keeping this line up—Hey you! What the hell you think you're doing? Those are dress pants! Try them on first, duffus! We don't want you going home on leave looking like the slobs you're gonna look like here ... hahah-hohohhahahahheeha!"

We were then issued an olive green laundry bag and trucked to another building on the other side of camp where a tall lanky supply sergeant drawled something about the issuance of combat equipment. "Open up your bags and my corporals will come around and issue you your field equipment which you will then place inside your green laundry bag. I will then call out the name of each piece of equipment at which point I want you to retrieve it from your green laundry bag and hold it up in the air so I can see it. Is that clear?"

"YES, SERGEANT!"

"You will address me as Supply Sergeant!"

"Yes, Supply Sergeant!" I shouted. Alone. There was a long period of silence as several drill corporals made their way through the sea of duds and duffuses to pounce on me with their epithets of threats and obscenities. The supply corporals waded through the ranks distributing our gear and we dropped it into the green laundry bags. Then began the inventory.

"Shelter half!" the supply sergeant shouted.

I rummaged through my bag while looking around me to see what it was that everyone else would be displaying. What was a shelter half, anyway? And which half was it? And which half of what? I was a yeshiva boy, so what did I know from shelter halves? And anyway, what good would half a shelter do? It was as good as no shelter at all, you'd think. And moreover, how were we supposed to know what all this equipment was called when we were just starting out? And furthermore, why was it that even though nothing had been taught to us yet, everyone but me knew exactly what a shelter half was, because everyone but me was holding up a shelter half?

I continued fumbling through my bag for the shelter half when the supply sergeant shouted "Helmet liner!" So I started looking for what would most likely be a helmet liner while looking up now and then to see what everyone else was already holding up. I pulled out what turned out to be the helmet pot itself and held it up when a drill corporal pounced on me and threw it back in, admonishing me that it hadn't been announced yet. What, is he deaf? They had indeed announced it. What else was it that my comrades-not-yet-in-arms had held up for the supply sergeant to see? And why did they call the helmet a "helmet liner" anyway? And why did *their* helmets look a lot different than *mine?*

"Mess kit! Spoon, knife and fork!"

I dug into the bag again while everyone around me had their mess kit out in one fell swoop, their utensils hanging smartly from a ring attached to the kit. I finally got mine out but the utensils dropped to the grass clankity clank clanking against each other and by the time I got them hooked to that ring on the mess kit the supply sergeant was calling out "Tent, pegs and poles!" I struggled to get the mess kit back into the bag and searched for the pegs and the tent and the poles and pulled out my poncho instead. "Poncho!" he shouted. I threw the poncho back in and pulled out my tent, then realized the difference and withdrew the poncho again and stuffed the tent back in and in the process the pegs and poles slipped out of the bag, and as I struggled to stuff them back inside, the poncho got tangled on one of the pegs and my glasses fell off. I squatted down to fetch my glasses and lost my balance, falling all over the half-spilling bag causing the mess kit to slip out and the utensils to scatter. My helmet rolled out from the bag as well and headed for the spit-shine boots of a nearby drill corporal who watched in bewilderment.

"Pistol belt! Magazine pouches! Canteen!"

I found the canteen and some kind of belt with holes in it, but magazine pouches? What was a magazine pouch and what would a soldier need with reading material in the battlefield anyway? Maybe for morale? I searched and searched, then looked up to see what it was supposed to look like but by the time I found the pouches the supply sergeant shouted "That's all for now!" and walked off. Instantly I began putting the spilt gear back into the green laundry bag while noticing how everyone else had all of their gear still on the grass. I felt proud of my ability to be quicker than they in packing my gear. OK, so maybe they knew what a shelter half was, but could they pack a laundry bag as fast as a yeshiva boy? fast enough to flee the enemy? Drill Sergeant Steamer approached me from behind and kicked the equipment out of my hands and all over the grass.

"WHAT THE HELL YOU THINK YOU'RE DOING, BOY!?"

"I was just packing my ..."

"DID YOU HEAR ANYBODY GIVE THE ORDER TO PACK ANYTHING?!"

"No, but I ... we ... they ..."

"YOU DON'T PEE UNLESS YOU'RE TOLD TO!! IS THAT CLEAR, BOY?!"

"Yes, Sergeant, but I wasn't peeing, I was ..."

"DRILL SERGEANT, BOY!!"

"Yes, Drill Sergeant Boy."

"THAT'S DRILL SERGEANT STEAMER, BOY!!"

"Yes, Drill Sergeant Steamer Boy."

"YOU SOME KIND OF WISE GUY?!! GIMME FIFTY, BOY!!"

"I don't carry that kind of cash, Drill Sergeant Steamer Boy."

That afternoon I was given the special assignment of cleaning out the grease pit with a government-issue teaspoon. I was to become very good at this.

> A teacher should tutor the student
> even a hundred times, until the student
> comprehends the lesson.
>
> **✒ Babylonian Talmud, Berachot**

After chow time, Master Drill Sergeant Inerderein ordered everyone to gather around my bunk and showed us how to make our beds. I didn't get it the first time. I didn't get it the second time. I didn't get it the third time. The fourth time I said I got it but really didn't. In fact, throughout my time in the army it remained more difficult for me to make my bed than to reassemble a rifle in the dark.

We were also shown how to arrange our gear in the footlocker and the wall locker and how to brass our buckles and shine our boots and hang our clothes. I didn't get any of it. I was still a yeshiva boy, trained since childhood to analyze everything intellectually, especially things that appeared alien to logic, such as the nuances of military discipline, like why a khaki shirt had to hang in front of, rather than in back of, a khaki trouser. (Or was it the other way around?) And why they called it such a filthy name like *kahki*.

My first Friday evening terrified me. It meant the approach of my first *shabbat*, or Sabbath, when no work is permitted, let alone basic combat training. I had by now mastered the art of keeping kosher by nibbling on fruits, raw vegetables, hard boiled eggs, and dry cereals. I had acclimated all the cadre and fellow trainees to my thrice-a-day prayer antics. But refusing to train Friday sundown through Saturday sundown? This was going to be challenging, as none of my other religious observances had gotten in the way of the program so far.

So Friday came and we were of course out in the field running in full gear with our M-14 rifles held high over our heads, screaming all kinds of terrible things and then marching up and down a dusty road singing obscene songs at the top of our lungs, led by lyricists with three or more stripes who wore Smokey the Bear hats. We marched left right left, left right left, gimme your left, gimme your right, left right left, left right left. I had never before learned the fine art of walking with your left foot first and then your right. I had always assumed it was inconsequential which foot you started out on. But I soon discovered that if I extended my right foot when the word "left" was announced, it seemed to throw everyone out of step, which made me realize how easy it would be to fell an entire company of soldiers. What struck me more than anything else during the long marching and running was how everyone's helmet sat on their head nice and snug while mine bounced up and down on my clean shaven head, clinking and clanking on my skull and on the rim of my eyeglasses. It would be another three weeks before I would discover what a helmet liner was.

"Sergeant!" I shouted from the ranks, panting and trying to keep in cadence and wondering how in the world I was going to get out of a march to return to camp for the proper observance of my sabbath.

"Sergeant!" I shouted from the ranks as Private Jesus Ruidoso came running by my side in his fifth circle around the entire company with his M-14 held high over his head shouting: "I will not call my M-14 a rifle, I will call it a weapon! I will not call my M-14 a rifle, I will call it a weapon!" I had heard about Jesus here and there even in my very sheltered Jewish upbringing, but this was the first time I'd ever actually met him. It finally made sense to me why a whole religion had been created around him.

"Sergeant!" I shouted from the ranks wondering whether I would be penalized for requesting to leave the ranks to go back and observe my sabbath accordingly, like maybe be sentenced to the same fate as Jesus, to circle the entire company in a run with my phylacteries held high over my head shouting: "I will not ask permission to keep my sabbath! I will not ask permission to keep my sabbath!"

"Sergeant!" I shouted from the ranks at the short stocky sergeant running alongside the nearest flank to where I was positioned and wondering if the whole troop would collapse in mid-run were I to abandon them now and step out of cadence in order to observe the holy sabbath.

Needless to say I got no response. And so we continued running into the sunset, the very sunset that was announcing that the sabbath was arriving sooner and sooner and that we were running in the opposite direction of the camp.

So I stepped out.

My people had done this often before throughout the centuries: stepping out, standing out, speaking out, and defying the status quo of whatever was going on in the moment, of whatever everyone else was doing. That's why we weren't very popular with the populace. We couldn't just go about following everyone else and doing what everyone else was doing, believing what everyone else was believing, worshipping what everyone else was worshipping. Nope. Not us. We always had to be different. Or so it appeared to those who weren't. But all we were trying to do was to be ourselves, not some-one else. And it cost us our lives over and over and over again. And now I had done it. I had literally stepped out of line. I had gone and made that historically fatal move and defied the social glob, the omnipotent force of the Holy Trend. I had challenged the entire United States Army and I didn't even have a single bullet. I had no idea where the *chutzpah* came from that empowered me to dare, but in the dust of the marching soldiers I saw the faces of the millions of Jewish women, men, and children who had done it before me, and they egged me on, filling me with courage to face the conse-quences of my impulsive response to what felt authentic inside of me, for what I had to do for the honor of the Holy Sabbath.

I had stepped out of line. It was in my blood. A drill sergeant was at my side in a moment ready to martyr one more member of my ancient, brazen people.

"What the hell's wrong with you, boy?!"

"I'm Jewish. I have to return to camp to observe my sabbath. I have to get to the Jewish chapel somehow and quick."

I did it. I said it. I stood up for my religion, for my tradition, for my heritage, my people. I braced myself for the archetypal wrath of Torquemada. I could take it. I *would* take it. Like so many of my people before me. I was ready. I shut my eyes and prepared for the worst.

"Go on, then, get your ass back to camp."

Huh? I was pissed. The one time—probably the only time in my whole life—that I was prepared to martyr myself for my beliefs, and this is what happens? Zilch? Get my ass back to camp? But what about the punishment? What about some kind of harrassment, at least, like maybe clean the grease pit? A month of KP? How's about painting the latrine with a toothbrush? Nothing. I watched the com-pany disappear down the dusty road, their screaming and obscene singing fading off into the distance. I turned around and headed quickly back to camp, stumbled wearily into the empty barracks and changed into some clean fatigues. There wasn't time to clean the rifle ... uh, the weapon ... and return it to the supply room, so I stored it in my wall locker and headed for the chapel.

The Jewish chapel was empty. The phone rang in a corner office and I heard someone answer it. It turned out to be the Chaplain, Captain Kaplan. Wow. Salvation was finally within reach. I would tell him my predicament. He would take care of me, give me sanctuary in the sanctuary, maybe also a nice pastrami on rye. I waited at the doorway to his office as he struggled to answer the phone.

"Chaplain Kaplan Captain ... uh ... Captain Chaplain Kap ... uh ... Chaplain Captain Kaplan ... hello? Hello! Hello?!" He hung up and I knocked on the open door.

Excuse me, my name is Gershon Winkler. I'm Orthodox. Any kosher food around here? What? How do you know I really keep kosher? Gimme some kosher food and I'll eat it, that's how. Aren't you the Jewish chaplain? Can't you help me out with kosher food supplies and maybe also explain to the sergeants about my needs as an Orthodox Jew? What? I shouldn't make waves? What do you mean? I'm in the army? I know I'm in the army. This is neither the time or the place to do Orthodox? You mean there's nothing you can do? I'm in the army now, not yeshiva? Columbia, South Carolina, not Brooklyn? Thank you for setting me straight. When I get out I'll be sure to look you up and join your congregation. Good shabbos.

I prayed, ate some gefilte fish out of a jar in the chapel kitchen and returned to the barracks to find everyone gathered around my wall locker. I made my way through the crowd of onlookers to find Drill Sergeant Steamer steaming as he went ransacking through my wall locker. When he became aware of my arrival he shoved my dusty M-14 into my chest. I was glad that I had removed the bayonet.

"Never ever EVER leave your weapon in your locker, boy! Do you understand me? Never EVER! And never ever EVER leave your weapon dirty! NEVER! DO YOU READ ME?"

I spent Saturday night and all of Sunday cleaning the grease pit, doing KP, and painting the latrine with a toothbrush.

Chapter Four

War and Peas

Everybody up! Fall out! First platoon all present and accounted for! Second platoon all present and accounted for! Third platoon one man on sick call! Fourth platoon all present and accounted for! Present arms! Order arms! Company dismissed!

Chow. What's for chow? Alright, line up here and keep it down! Hey, Winkler, you better eat somethin', man. Yeah, man, where that dude goin'? Him? He's going to the barracks to eat that kosher shit he keeps in his locker. He Jewish, no? Yeah. Hell, I always thought them dudes had horns. Yeah, me, too. Reckon they must've cut 'em off when they give him his haircut. Yeah, must've. Alright keep it down!

It was the next morning, or maybe the morning after that. It could have been any one of a number of mornings that began the moment I would fall asleep. I did my prayer thing and munched on some matzoh I'd picked up at the Jewish chapel, and a can of peas I'd taken from the mess hall. It seemed like I was always hungry and never full, sustaining myself with dry cereal, milk, matzoh, and canned peas. Drill Sergeant Streamer came in to tell me to start waxing the floor. That way, I figured, we could have a shiny clean floor to come back to at sunset, and to tread over in muddy boots and stuff.

I waxed the floor and buffed it without losing control of the machine.

Fall out! Company ten hut! Forward harsh! Left, right, left. Left, right, left. Left, right, left. Left, right, left. Gimme your right. RIGHT! Gimme your left. LEFT! Left, right, left. Left, right, left. Oh, gimme your left, left, left right left. Gimme your left, left, your left right left.

Left, left, left right left. Your left, your left, your left right left. Column right forwaaard—tarsh! Left, right, left. Left, right, left.

Lest the reader come away with the impression that marching was boring, I shall recount here a typical song that often accompanied our strolls through the woods of South Carolina, sung to the cadence of left, right, left.

"I don't know but I've been told!" Drill Sergeant Streamer would sing.

"I DON'T KNOW BUT I'VE BEEN TOLD!" we would sing in response.

"This Fort Jackson's mighty old!"

"THIS FORT JACKSON'S MIGHTY OLD!"

"Am I right or wrong?!"

"YOU'RE RIGHT!" (while stepping down with the right foot)

"Am I going strong?!"

"YOU'RE RIGHT!"

"Sound off!"

"ONE TWOOOOOOO, THREE FOUUUUUUR, ONE, TWO, THREE, FOUR, ONE TWO THREE FOUR!"

"Your mother was there when you left!"

"YOU'RE RIGHT!"

"You're girlfriend was there when you left!"

"YOU'RE RIGHT!"

"Oh, what'll I find when I get back?!"

"WHAT'LL I FIND WHEN I GET BACK?!"

"Jody's got my cadillac!"

"JODY'S GOT MY CADILLAC!"

"I'm out here all alone!"

"I'M OUT HERE ALL ALONE!"

"Jody's got my girl and gone!"

"JODY'S GOT MY GIRL AND GONE!"

"Am I right or wrong?!"

"YOU'RE RIGHT!"

"Am I going strong?!"

"YOU'RE RIGHT!"

"Sound off ..."

"ONE TWOOOOOOO, THREE FOUUUUUUR, ONE, TWO, THREE, FOUR, ONE TWO THREE FOUR!"

Rifle range.

I climbed down into foxhole number 12, designated to me by a drill corporal. And then another drill corporal came by and ordered me to another foxhole so that a left-handed recruit could use mine. I climbed down into the other foxhole and waited for the instructions to bellow out of the loudspeaker sitting way up on the control tower behind me.

"Nu, Gershon." It was the soft Hebraic voice of my Rosh Yeshiva in Jerusalem admonishing me in his gentle old rabbinic way, smiling from behind his thinning white beard, his eyes twinkling that wise and ancient twinkle. "So is *this* the purpose of life? Would it not have been more purposeful to have stayed in Jerusalem studying the holy Torah and working on your character, rather than to be wasting your time with this *naarishkeit?* Ayiyiyiyiyi. Gershon Gershon Gershon. The Evil Inclination has succeeded where we have failed. Yesterday you were sitting in the yeshiva swaying back and forth in ecstasy reviewing the instructions of the holy writ and blissing out on the Holy Blessed One, and today you're sitting in a foxhole in the rain staring at artificial targets and awaiting eagerly the instructions of a Hittite. Ayiyiyiyiyiyi. Gershon Gershon Gershon."

"We'll start firing as soon as the duffus on number 14 gets into the correct foxhole position!"

It was the lieutenant in the tower. My Rosh Yeshiva faded away, shaking his head slowly from side to side. I frowned. What could I say? He was right. But there were other dimensions to life that I needed to experience than swaying to and fro with the holy books all day. And furthermore ...

"We're waiting for number 14 to get into the correct foxhole position!"

... anyway, furthermore, I had spent so many years in my head, studying Talmud, thinking through commentative *pilpul,* researching halachic dicta, praying, analyzing, midrashing—it was time I got like down into my body. And ...

"Number 14, we're still waiting. It's nice and warm up here in the tower."

... and doing this army thing felt like a very important process of doing just that, of getting from my head back into my body, back into the moment, into real life ...

"Number 14 goddammit if you don't get your shit together in the next ten seconds I'll have this entire company out here all night long with no breaks!"

... and into down-to-earth activities, because here and now I was being forced by circumstance to pay attention, to become alert to my surroundings, to take responsibility for my actions and inactions, to ...

"Number 14!! I'll have your ass welded into that foxhole for the rest of your time in the army if you don't assume the correct foxhole position NOW!!!"

... to respond to what's happening around me, you know? Take for instance the poor *schmeggeg* in foxhole number 14. I've been hearing this guy get bellowed at from the tower for ten minutes now and he still can't get it together. Now this hapless *schlemiel* is a prime example of someone stuck in their head and plain unable to get into their body.

"Number 14!! You've got to the count of ten to wake up or you're in shit deeper than that foxhole!!!"

I looked up and down the foxhole line and joined my comrades-in-arms in their frustration over having to wait in a cold, damp foxhole for this *schmuck* to get his act together. It was getting colder and the rain was falling harder and we hadn't even gotten off our first round.

" ... three, four, five ... "

Now I, too, was growing impatient with whoever number 14 was. My feet were getting numb and my ears were tingling. If that idiot would only get into the correct position we could get our break soon and retreat to that nice big tent behind the tower where they had set up a kerosene stove for warmth.

"… eight, nine …! I'm warning you, everyone's gonna be out here an extra two hours today if you don't act now!!"

That did it! Why should I and the others suffer because of some dumb *yold* who forgot how to assume the correct foxhole firing position after a whole week of learning it? I began to scour the range in search of who this pitiful character might be. I scanned the numbers on the targets, which corresponded to the numbers on the foxholes. I caught sight of target number 17 and then began following the targets down the line to number 14.

It was me.

Suddenly, a pack of drill corporals wielding wooden safety signals shaped like ping-pong rackets converged upon me. The wooden safety rackets came down hard on my helmet pot which bounced up and down and all around on my head. I began to wonder what the significance of the helmet was anyway if it couldn't protect the head. Meanwhile, my head was vibrating and my ears were ringing and my eyeglasses were embedded in the bridge of my nose and dangling loosely from my ears. One of the corporals man-handled me into the correct foxhole firing position and then the cadre departed as mysteriously as they had arrived.

After about an hour of firing the lieutenant shouted "Cease fire!" but I didn't understand the terminology, so I squeezed off one more round.

"Number fourteen!!" the lieutenant shouted angrily. In response, I turned around to face the tower to see what he wanted, now that I knew who number fourteen was. The lieutenant ducked and a cadre of corporals pounced all over me once more, first knocking the front of my weapon away so that it was pointed away from the tower, and then beating their rackets all over whatever was left of my helmet.

After the corporals had left, a stocky African American sergeant approached and crouched down at the opening of the foxhole, studying my helmet in astonishment. He was the same sergeant who had shocked me on Friday by releasing me to return to camp to observe my Sabbath.

"Lemme ask you somethin', Private."

"Yes, Sergeant. I mean, Drill Sergeant. I mean, Drill Sergeant Zopes."

"Where the fuck is your helmet liner?"

That day I learned what a helmet liner was. It was this kind of a helmet-shaped insert that fit into the helmet pot and served the purpose of absorbing any shock to the head, such as the blows from safety rackets wielded by drill corporals. Drill Sergeant Zopes introduced me to one and showed me how to adjust it so that my helmet no longer bopped up and down when I walked.

The days continued with no gap in between, waxing floors, buffing floors, running in full gear, marching, rifle range, sand pits, hand-to-hand combat, bayonet practice, and peas. In the morning I'd have cold cereal, in the afternoon I would have matzoh and peas, sometimes some fruit, and in the evening a cold can of Hebrew National braised rice with beef procured from the Jewish chapel. In the field, I would do my prayer three times daily no matter what we were doing. We could be on the firing range or in grenade practice, but when the sun started sinking it was *minchah* time and I'd stop what I was doing and recite my afternoon prayer. On Friday nights and Saturdays I would hang out at the chapel to do my Sabbath, sometimes missing important training, and always missing the physical combat proficiency tests which were held only on Saturdays.

Then one day, while I was cleaning out my rifle, Drill Sergeant Zopes called me into his cadre room. He was all cleaned up and sharply dressed for an overnight pass and was shining his shoes when I walked in. Merv was there, too, a frail Jewish guy who had been playing with the philharmonic or something when he'd suddenly gotten drafted. Merv was a gentle, sensitive man about five years my senior with a wife and kid back in New York. What happened to him was exactly what I'd joined the army to avoid: being separated from the wife and kids.

Sergeant Zopes put on his shiny black shoes, tied them tight, and then got down to business. First he turned to Merv.

"Merv, you failed your Combat Proficiency Test. The Captain's ordered you recycled. You're goin' to Special Training Camp for two weeks. At the end of that period you will be given another test. If you pass it, you'll be reassigned to another company in their third or fourth week to continue your basic training program. So pack your bags and be waitin' out in front tomorrow morning at 0700 hours."

Merv left without a word. He was a musician. To him, life was probably one big symphony. Everything was orchestrated. Eventually, things would reach a crescendo and climax. And then he'd be back with his family in New York, with one more day at Carnegie Hall tucked neatly behind him.

"Same with you, Winkler," Zopes continued. "Pack up and be ready at 0700 tomorrow. A truck will take you and Merv to Special Training Camp."

I protested. I had improved a lot. I could run like everyone else. I could hit some of the targets finally. I could flip an attacker if he was a foot shorter than me. I could crawl a hundred yards in sixty seconds. I could disassemble my rifle in the dark. At times I could even put it back together again in the light.

"Look, Winkler, I'm aware of all that."

"So why am I being recycled?"

He stood up and put on his ribbon-decorated dress jacket. He wasn't looking at me. There was obviously something going on that he was not pleased with, that he felt was unfair, but about which he was helpless to do anything.

"The CO isn't happy about you skippin' out on the PT test last Saturday."

"But I made it clear to the First Sergeant that Saturday's my Sabbath and that I'd gladly take the test any other time."

"I know that. But the cap'n don't like the way you're puttin' your religion above your training. He don't like freaks in the company. Understand what I'm sayin'? He wants everything to be even and smooth and no special favors or exceptions and stuff like that, understand? Otherwise it shows up on his records and … look, I'll go over and talk to him for you, but I can't guarantee nothin'. The old man's up for promotion at the end of the cycle, so he might not want to do anything that might get in the way of it, you see?"

Zopes was gone and back in half an hour. He looked like he had gotten yelled at. I thanked him anyway for trying. The captain wanted a clean company. No room for individuals, he explained. No room for matzoh balls and prayer shawls. This was about war, not peas.

Dear Mother and Father:

Everything is fine. Sorry I haven't written in a while but I'm in a special training unit and we're very busy here with important training. Needless to say, not everyone gets to go to Special Training. I was among only two who were selected out of four hundred men. Anyway, everything is okay otherwise. Kosher food is plentiful here and there's no problem with keeping the Sabbath or with praying three times a day. The people here are very nice. We go hiking a lot and camp out sometimes and do target practice and other games. There's no pool though. Regards to the family. See you soon, maybe for Chanukah.

Love, Gershon

I'm not going to bore you further with the army portion of my story. I mean, Special Training Camp was uneventful. What can I tell you about it? We slept in tents although it was a cold and bitter winter, they woke us up in the middle of the night to harrass us, make us waddle like ducks around the tents, or carry our foot lockers on our backs, sometimes our mattresses. It was a two-week program of physical and emotional stress designed to break the most problematic trainees, ranging from criminal elements, the obese, sociopaths, psychopaths, and Danish-born Jews who wouldn't train on Saturday.

One glitch. To get out of Special Training Camp you had to pass their own version of the combat proficiency test. And of course, these tests were given only on Saturdays. So, Saturday after Saturday I refused to take the test and remained in Special Training Camp for several cycles, longer than the sociopaths, psychopaths and criminal elements who after two weeks were ready to do anything to get out. Finally, a young lieutenant noticed my ever present presence, examined my records and summoned me to his office.

"I notice you've been here longer than some of the cadre."

"Yes, sir."

"You've been here longer than me."

"Yes, sir."

"Don't you want to leave this place?"

"Yes, sir."

"Well, then, why won't you just put aside your religious observances for just one weekend and free yourself of this place?"

"I can only trespass my Sabbath if there was danger to health or life, sir."

"How's your health?"

"Excellent, sir."

"So, you're prepared to remain at Special Training Camp for the duration of your stay in the army if need be if it means violating your Sabbath to get out."

"Yes, sir."

"I know lots of Jews in the army who put their religious observances on hold until they cleared all the mandatory training programs."

"Yes, sir."

There was a pause for what seemed to be a long period of time. The lieutenant wrote some notes on a pad and then dismissed me. The following Sunday a sergeant was assigned to administer a private combat proficiency test for me. I passed with flying colors and was released from Special Training Camp and reassigned to the fourth week of a regular outfit to finish my eight-week basic training program. My records now ordered that any Saturday tests be administered to me on alternate days, and so it was. By the time I got out of basic training, I was the most proficiently trained soldier the United States Army had ever had, having received four times more basic training than any other soldier in history.

There really isn't any need to describe my entire military experience like advanced infantry training and the remainder of my service. I'm not one of those sore loser veterans who go about looking for ways to get people to feel sorry for them, like by telling about their horrendous experiences in the army or at war. Face it, the average mother has gone through a helluva lot more terror, pain, and facing-death-straight-in-the-eye, than most vets with Purple Hearts emblazoned on their license plates. Place a war hero in a delivery room of a maternity ward and watch him go limp or pass out. War is hell, but giving birth is harder.

Listen, I don't mean to digress from my story, this book, but I really got to get this off my chest: Men are such babies, I swear. Big heroes, big macho heroes they are for going off to some war where civilian women and kids face the same dangers but without any awards or hometown parades. What men don't realize is that it's men who start those damn wars to begin with. And yet we're supposed to feel sorry for them when they come home from a shoot-out that was no more traumatic than your average daily shoot-out on your average urban street corner.

War and Peas

So, I'm not going to tell you about how hard it was for me in the army trying to keep kosher and observe the Sabbath and pray three times a day and soldier along the hazardous 38th parallel of the DMZ in South Korea during biting cold winter storms blowing fiercely through the wilds of the Manchurian mountains. Nor will I discuss how hard it was for me to decline offers of fellow soldiers to pay for me to get laid in "Turkey Village." Or what it was like not being able to feel your toes and fingers while walking guard duty in the dead of winter, or getting shot at and shooting back at barely visible flashes of gunfire hundreds of yards away, wondering what wondering used to be like. Or being a Chaplain's Assistant to some jerk who spent more time polishing the brass on his shoulders than the brass on the Torah scrolls. Or schlepping all over the DMZ to do Sabbath services because the new chaplain didn't want to carry a .45 which was required up there. Or sitting all Sabbath day long in a frozen pup tent with my M-14 rifle because army regulations forbade me to leave it unattended and Jewish regulations forbade me to carry it on the Sabbath unless I was getting shot at, and no one was shooting that Saturday. Or walking by the corpse of a baby girl thrown into the frozen Imjin River for economic reasons. Or massaging Zimmerman's frostbitten foot inside my armpit in the dead of night, miles from base while on a lost patrol.

These are not the kinds of things I feel necessary to talk about. I am not that kind of veteran. I served my country, albeit in someone else's country, then turned in my guns, hung up my combat boots, got my discharge, had some free dental work done and finished! Nor will I bore you with the trauma of discovering that I could have served only two years instead of three had I specified that I was *volunteering for the draft* instead of *joining*. So while others who volunteered went home in 1969, I went home in 1970 because no one told me you could volunteer for the draft and serve only two years like any other draftee instead of three years like a *schlemiel.*

For fourteen months in Korea I lived on peas and rice. Peas and rice, peas and rice, peace and rice. Also there was an occasional treat of rice and peas. Sometimes I had rice and peas instead. Kosher options were few in Korea besides fruits, veggies, milk, cheese, peas and rice, rice being the only hot meal.

But I survived and came home, embraced my parents, and sat down for my first decent hot kosher meal in eons. Yet, as happy as my mother was to see me, she carried a lot of grief around my having gone to the army without her.

"I was so worried. I said *tehilim* (Psalms) every day and night. I cried every time I saw the news about Vietnam ..."

"I was in Korea."

"Korea, Vietnam, it's all the same thing to a mother. How could you go to the army? Didn't you care about how I felt? Didn't you think I would be worrying about you day and night? Tell me, were you really dafted, or did you join? Tell me the truth."

"Join? Ha! How could you think such a thing? With the Vietnam war raging, you could even think such a thing, that I joined? I told you already. I was called."

"Then why didn't we ever see the letter? Why suddenly do we find out that you have to report to Fort Jackson?"

"They work fast."

"But why didn't you show us the letter?"

"I didn't want to worry you."

"Ha! Believe me, I worried plenty. You could have gone back to Denmark. You're still a Danish citizen."

"There's no anti-Semitism there."

"You could have gone back to yeshiva and dodged the draft that way."

"Why are we going through all this now that I'm home and out of the army? It's over!"

"Over? For *you* it's over. For me, your mother, it goes on, all the scars in my heart from worrying day and night. I said *tehilim* for you every day."

"And night."

"And night. Yes. And every time the news came on about Vietnam ..."

"I was in Korea."

"Korea, Vietnam, it's the same."

"The Korean war ended a long time ago."

"For me it started the day you landed there. Don't tell me nothing was going on there."

"Nothing was going on there."

"There was no shooting?"

"There was, but not much more than in your average American city on a weekend."

"I am sure it was worse than that. You just won't tell me."

"It's over. It doesn't matter. I'm alive and well and home and hungry."

"I made a special supper for your homecoming."

"Thanks. What did you make?"

"Peas and rice."

Chapter Five

Nest Quest

It is written: "It was very good" (Genesis 1:31). Said Rabbi Nach'mon ben Sh'muel, "The reference is to the Evil Inclination. But is the Evil Inclination *very good?* Indeed it is so, for were it not for the Evil Inclination, a man would not build a house or take a wife or beget a child, or work."

⚬⚬ Midrash B'reishis Rabbah 9:9

One day I became a man. You know: ready for marriage, kids, a job, and an apartment in Brooklyn. No sooner had my mother finished burning my military uniform, when she set out to find me a woman who would keep me from joining the French Foreign Legion.

I also had a job, so now I could get married and raise a family. When I'd returned home from military life, I had taken one of those silly aptitude tests offered by the career guidance people at the Veterans Administration, and the social worker had advised me to go into teaching or community work. What a joke, I thought as I'd left the VA building. Me a teacher? Me doing community stuff? Give me a break. Neither was of any interest to me. Heck, if I wanted to be a rabbi I'd have accepted rabbinic ordination from the sweet elderly *Rosh Yeshiva* back in Jerusalem. Anyway, I didn't need no aptitude test or guidance counselor to tell me what I was good at. I wanted to be a writer. So much for their ludicrous testing system.

Indeed, within a week I landed a job as a writer for McGraw-Hill Book Company. Just goes to show you how incompetent those VA career counselors are. Yessir, within a week I was writing alright. I was writing names and addresses on envelopes. Okay, okay, so I wasn't a real writer right away, just a kind of velveteen sort of writer, but eventually I ended up assisting the editor-in-chief of the Imported Books Department and he gave me my first break, allowing me to write press releases and stuff, and evaluating manuscripts. Tom Quinn was his name, and to this day I owe him a debt of gratitude for sparking my career as a writer even though I still haven't made a penny from it yet. Two years with Tom led me to an opening in the educational books division where I landed a position as a promotional copywriter, and thus I became a real, live, genuine professional writer.

Of course I also dated. I was set up with one Orthodox Jewish woman after another, but they seemed to find me peculiar, not quite right, not quite the kind of yeshiva guy they had in mind. None of them could fathom what the heck I had been doing in the army. And during a war, yet. Sure, they admired me for my unrelenting observance of religious strictures and practices while serving those three long years, but WHY? Why did you end up in the army? So I changed my story a little. I got drafted, I told them. My rationale for enlisting had fallen on deaf ears all around. So from then on I just told everyone that I'd been drafted, that I'd been a helpless victim of systematic inductions by the Czarist regime of pure and innocent yeshiva boys into a rigid and hazardous military run by and composed of gentiles who used dirty language.

My new story worked to some degree. The dates lasted longer. One girl almost touched my upper left arm, through my jacket and shirt, of course. Orthodox dating does not include touching and necking and kissing. In fact, we were never in a private situation where such sins could occur. Always it was either in public settings or in either party's apartment with the door opened to a public thoroughfare. It's not that there is anything technically wrong with a single Jewish man touching a single Jewish woman. In fact, there is nothing technically wrong with a *married* Jewish man touching a single Jewish woman, or with a married Jewish *woman* touching a single Jewish man or a *married* Jewish man. Only, the rabbis, bless them, instituted fences around intimacy to prevent the inevitable one-thing-leads-to-another syndrome. But in non-intimate contexts like doctoring, or like rescuing a drowning woman married to someone else, or sitting on a bus next to a naked woman, or shaking hands socially—touch is not an issue except to those who choose to take the laws beyond their original limitations.

Dating, however, constitutes a context of intimacy. And while Judaism has no actual legislation against nonmarital sex, single people still don't hold hands or neck or kiss because while single sex is not forbidden, sex with a menstruant woman is. And a menstruant woman is not only a woman who is bleeding from the womb, but also a woman who has completed her period and has not yet immersed herself in a ritual pool of naturally gathered waters, or *mikveh*. And single people don't go to the *mikveh* because they don't have cause since it is presumed that they have no sexual partners. And therefore single women are presumed always to be in the state of the menstruant woman and forbidden sexually to a Jewish man. It's just an assumption, you see, but practiced as if it were law. Of course, a single Jewish woman *could* immerse herself after her period and have legitimate sexual relations with her boyfriend without violating anything. But the communal *mikveh* is set up so that only married women are welcome, except for a single woman about to be married or a single woman undergoing conversion, or a single woman lying through her teeth about her being married. This safeguard prevents single sex from happening, a measure without basis in Jewish law but which was adopted by Jewry since the early middle ages in response to the forced morality of the Church, a morality that had zero tolerance for the stuff Judaism tolerated such as polygamy and living together, which were both common and acceptable in Jewish practice from ancient times. So some single women who are observant of Jewish law simply head for the beach or a lake or to a rare communal *mikveh* that *will* allow them to immerse.

Anyway, in my community the party-line was no touch. Just nice
dates with cordial discussions about family, values, ideology, religion, personal life history, and cuisine. Sometimes you match, sometimes not.

One *Shabat*, while my mother was out hunting in the wilds of
Rabbi Shainblum's modest little *shtib'l* (sort of a basement synagogue), she was moved by the angelic devotion of an attractive petite
woman I will call Bryna in this story in order to protect her real name
which, again, happens also to be Bryna, but by pure coincidence.

Bryna was very devout, a major reason why I chose to marry her.
I wanted to be so devout, so orthodoxic, that the Evil Inclination
would gag and leave me alone for good. I had put the army behind
me, still had never had sexual intercourse, was 23 years old, and
had even refrained from the sin of masturbation. I had made it. I
was intact. I was holy, but I knew that I'd never really be safe from
the Evil Inclination unless I surrendered my soul into the hands of a
woman so staunch in her religious convictions that her influence
would repel the Evil One like bug spray.

So I got married to Bryna and lived happily ever after and begat
three beautiful daughters. And I would ride the crowded, noisy sub-
ways like everyone else during rush hour and go to work every morning and come home every night to the safety of my kosher orthodoxic
haven, safe from the grips of the Evil Inclination. Bryna became my
guardian angel, and the Evil One trembled in her pious presence.

> Rabbi Chiyya (2nd century) was constantly tormented
> by his wife. Yet, whenever he came upon something
> that might be pleasing to her, he wrapped it in his
> turban and brought it home. One day, his colleague,
> Rav, noticed that he was wrapping a gift for his wife
> and asked: "But why? She is always tormenting the
> master!" Replied Rabbi Chiyya: "It is enough that they
> rear our children and save us from sin."
>
> **Babylonian Talmud, *Y'vamot* 63a**

And so it came to pass that in the summer of 1975, publishing companies were experiencing a severe drought in their cash flow, especially in educational books departments, and many were laid off, including me. And so, with my new portfolio of professional writing, manuscript evaluation and copyediting, I went looking for work and ultimately decided that I would freelance. What better places to freelance for a nice Orthodox Jewish boy, I thought, than *Jewish* publishers? In no time I had freelance copyediting work to take home from Shengold Publishers and from Hebrew Publishing Company.

> The Evil Inclination is likened at first
> to the thread of a spider's web,
> and in the end becomes
> as powerful as a boat's rope.
>
> **Babylonian Talmud, *Sukah* 52a**

Okay. Now it begins. The Evil Inclination had designed an incredibly clever scheme to get at me in the most roundabout way, circumventing the moat that Bryna had forged around me. So listen carefully.

One day, the editor-in-chief at Hebrew Publishing Company handed me a manuscript to copyedit. It was authored by a former vice president of the Board of Jewish Education of Greater New York. I took the job home and went to work. When I'd completed the editing, it was reviewed by the author who then met with me to discuss the possibility of my becoming the Book Editor for the Board of Jewish Education. He felt I'd be good at it and that they sorely needed one. So I took the job, glad to have a secure position once again with a predictable paycheck.

Not a year went by before a phone call to the education department was misdirected to my office under the guidance of you-know-who.

"My name is Robin and I'm calling from Massapequa."

"And how may I be of help? You found a typo in one of our books? I had nothing to do with that book. It was probably that Hungarian fella …"

"Oh no no no, I'm not calling about any books. I'm calling about missionaries."

"I'm sorry, we don't proselytize. But if you called our …"

"May I finish?"

"Finish? I'm sorry, let me be quiet and hear what it is you're calling about."

"Thank you. Okay, our community is …"

"You know, it reminds me of a teaching in the Talmud: 'The arrogant cannot teach, and the shy cannot learn.' So anyway, I will now be quiet and let you say your piece."

"Thank you. Our community is …"

"I think that's in the Babylonian Talmud, in the tractate of *Avot*, chapter two, *Mishnah* number five. Would you like me to send you a xerox of that?"

"No, thank you. So, our community is being bombarded with missionary flyers aimed at luring our teenagers to these so-called Hebrew Christian coffee houses and activities."

"Oh, you mean those 'Jews for Jesus' people?"

"No, these are well-organized groups out here on the island who have set up what they call 'synagogues' where they draw big crowds of Jewish teens and young adults to their worship services, with Jewish symbols and decorations all over the place, and they play Hebrew songs on the record player, and then they sneak in prayers to Jesus and teachings about Christianity. I have been trying to call Jewish organizations around the city for help in dealing with this and the Federation directed me to the Board of Jewish Education and now I'm talking to you. Can you help?"

What was I supposed to do? As an ultra-Orthodox *yeshiva* man I could not allow this call to fall into the hands, God forbid, of my colleagues who were mostly Reform and Conservative. Even the few pedagogic specialists who were Orthodox were *modern* Orthodox, too compromising, I felt. This case had to be handled by the Real McCoy, the authentic and true-blue representatives of Torah Judaism. And I was the only agent of that quality of Jewishness available at the Board of Jewish Education. In a flash, I turned from Book Editor to community outreach worker. In a flash, the face of the guidance counselor at the VA office flickered before my eyes laughing at me heartily. In a flash, I realized that this was a holy call, urgent work in the service of God and for the survival of the Jewish peoplehood. And I knew that I had to respond before some gung-ho Reform or Conservative outreach person could, so that the Orthodox community could have first crack at rescuing these hapless suburban Jews from assimilation and proselytizing, and ultimately make them all Orthodox.

"Well," I finally said to the woman on the phone. "I will help you. First, gather together members of your community, parents, leaders, whomever, and then call me back and we'll set up a date and time to meet and I will bring to you some experts who will help you out."

There was a pause for what seemed to be a long period of time.

"You mean this is it? No more run-arounds? No more calls to make? You will actually just come out here and help us?"

"Absolutely. As is written in the Babylonian Talmud: 'In a situation where there is no one doing what needs to be done, you be the one to do it' (Babylonian Talmud, *Avot* 2:5)."

"Could you send me a xerox of that?"

"I'm sorry, but the machine is down."

Barely a week later I found myself coordinating a community meeting in Massapequa, Long Island between distraught parents, concerned leadership, and my quickly gathered entourage of representatives from Orthodox Jewish outreach organizations. I spoke, they spoke, we spoke. In the end, the Jews of Massapequa were promised our help. But not until they had heard my candid tirade on why it was that their kids were so susceptible to the lure of the Hebrew Christian coffee houses and worship services.

"Your children are starving. Their souls are yearning for spirituality, the one nutrient you haven't fed them; the one nutrient missing from the worship menu at your mausoleum-like temple and from the curriculum of your once-a-week sham of Jewish education you call 'Sunday School', not to mention the travesty of your Bar/Bat-Mitzvah factories. No surprise, then, that they flock now to these places where they are singing, not reciting; where they are rejoicing, not *krechtzing*; where they are being given meaning to their lives, not excuses. All of what they seek there, we have had all along in our own rich and ancient tradition, but not even *you* have known or learned about it or practiced it in your homes and in your daily lives, so how do you expect your kids to know that what they are seeking exists in their own tradition?"

I suggested the establishment of a coffee house for young Jewish adults, a place to socialize, to be exposed to Jewish experience and learning, and free of anything remotely resembling the very institutions that had turned them off to begin with. It had to be community sponsored, run by grass-roots folks, concerned parents, and me.

Thus was born the Jewish coffee house phenomenon on Long Island, spreading from community to community like wildfire, from Massapequa to North Bellmore to East Meadow to Oceanside to Woodmere to Ronkonkoma to Stony Brook—even one in Manhattan for Russian Jewish immigrants—successfully luring young Jewish adults away from those who lured them away from us.

Then there was the coffeehouse program I had helped to start in Manhattan for newly arrived Soviet Jewish immigrants. I would teach Judaism to these spiritually starved young women and men and do some Hebrew numbers on the guitar to liven things up. I would also help them find furniture, housing, maybe a job and stuff like that. One evening the participants whispered to me that there was a famous comedian in the coffeehouse. I looked up and saw a depressed looking young man with a short-cropped beard lingering in a corner of the room. I had met Russian physicians and professors whose lives shifted dramatically to an all-time low upon their arrival in the states, as many had become taxi drivers and building custodians to make ends meet. And here, alas, was a Russian comedian down on his luck.

I summoned Yaakov to the circle and let him know that I had been informed he was a comedian back in the USSR. He responded shyly, and when I asked him to tell us all some jokes, he became withdrawn. There was this sense of sadness, like what's the point? He was through. He'd never make it here as a comedian. He'd left that behind when he chose to leave Russia. But I persisted. The man needed to tell a joke. He needed priming so that maybe he would at least dream about doing comedy in the states. So he broke down and told a joke. We laughed. It was a good joke, and the delivery— broken English and all—was superb. I asked for another joke. He told another, this time with more *umph* than the first. More laughter. I didn't have to ask for yet another joke because Yaakov was warming up. Comedy was still a possibility. I felt good about making him feel better, and then he slipped my mind altogether amid so many other people and projects with which I had become involved.

The coffee houses of course drew the attention of the Hebrew Christian missionaries who attempted to infiltrate but with no success. In fact, one of their best men became in the end one of ours. Some of the otherwise assimilated attendees and parent coordinators are at this writing ultra-Orthodox Jews in full regalia and practice, and others went off to Israel to study and enrich their lives with their heritage that had until then been a mystery to them. One of the Reform rabbis on the island even asked me to study with him, to reintroduce him to the tradition that had been paved over by his movement in its well-meaning but dismally failed attempt over the past two centuries to assimilate Judaism into western European and American "modernity."

Tragically, though, the people I'd bring down to the coffee houses from Orthodox outreach organizations were impotent in their attempts to stir Jewish spiritual awareness or interest in these young people whose primary concerns were rock'n roll and sex, plus a little meaning on the side. Realizing that no one I was bringing was capable of reaching them, I decided to try one final, yet un-tried program: me. Until then I'd been coordinating, bringing others to teach or sing or speak. In the process, I'd noticed how the youth had taken a liking to me, so I thought I'd give it a shot. It worked. They listened. Somehow, I had the right tempo, the right lingo, the right timing, the right jokes, the right words. Before I knew it, I was sending people to Jerusalem to study for a year at any one of increasing numbers of *ba'alei t'shuvah yeshivot*—Orthodox academies of Jewish studies geared toward those raised with little or no background. This was during the late seventies and early eighties, the great age of cults, deprogrammings, seekers of the meaning of life. From answering a single, misdirected phone call, I had become an important part of the great age of spiritual seeking.

I had become a rabbi and didn't know it.

Of course, the Board of Jewish Education gobbled up the publicity from such successful endeavors and accomplishments by their Book Editor, and in turn granted me some funds to cover my expenses while I was launching these coffee houses, happy to have their name on flyers and in articles as co-sponsors and to brag at board meetings of their pet project "Priority One."

But the BJE's honeymoon lasted only a few months, when the YMHA of Long Island complained to the New York Federation of Jewish Philanthropies, who ran both the Jewish "Y" and the BJE. Their complaint was simply that what I was doing was their domain, not that of the BJE. They were the ones who ought to be sponsoring this project, not the Board of Jewish Education, and certainly it ought not to be run by a book editor but by a social worker from the YMHA! The Federation then handed me the ultimatum: hand over the coffee houses to the "Y" and stick to book editing, or hand over the coffee houses to the "Y" and work for *them*.

For me, it was clear that neither choice was feasible. I could not give up this important and holy outreach work that had become so successful, nor could I affiliate it with the very institutions responsible for alienating our youth with their empty programs and soul-less activities. I was left with no other choice but to quit and go back to freelancing for a living while running the coffee houses.

But other organizations had caught wind of the coffee house rage and soon I was contacted by the Union of Orthodox Jewish Congregations of America and offered a full-time position as their collegiate coordinator. I would do the coffee houses under their auspices and sponsorship and also be responsible for outreach to unaffiliated Jewish students on various campuses. Everything was going my way. As it is written: "In the way a person wishes to go, they are led" (Babylonian Talmud, *Makot* 10b).

I now went beyond the coffee houses to man an outreach table at the State University of New York at Stony Brook, where I ended up debating scriptures with the Campus Crusade for Christ and the Jews For Jesus people whose table stood next to mine. Within four months of bible-babbling and scriptural ping-pong, I sent the head of the campus based Jews-for-Jesus to Jerusalem where she attended a women's yeshiva and turned Orthodox within a year. Pastor after pastor was dispatched to argue scripture with me but to no avail. I was good. I knew my stuff. I was going to save Jewry from Christian proselytizing aimed specifically at Jews. For centuries my people had stood their ground against forced conversions and had given up their lives rather than accept the Christian faith, and now the bloodied sword of past crusades had been replaced by the guise of loving and compassionate outreach aimed at the unassuming, unlearned, and otherwise alienated young Jewish adult. Once again my people were being burned at the stake, this time spiritually, and guys and gals like me rose to the occasion to bring our sisters and brothers back to the fold.

One night, the UOJCA people came down to visit one of my coffee houses, to kind of see me at work. To their shock, they found guys with girls on their laps, girls in immodest attire, guys not wearing yarmulkas or any other head coverings. I was called to task. I was reminded that my coffee houses were under their auspices and sponsorship, which meant that everything had to go according to Orthodox practice. What was going on in that basement in Massapequa violated everything down the line. This had to change, I was told.

I knew it couldn't change without alienating the already alienated, and that the rabbis at the UOJCA had no idea of what it took to bring back to Judaism those who entertained not so much as a smidgen of interest in it. So I quit the UOJCA and once again took the coffee house movement with me, not about to jeopardize this highly effective and holistic outreach mode for the sake of organizational politics or religious protocol.

Ohr Somayach picked me up next, one of those institutions in Jerusalem that had sprung up during the sixties to take advantage of the Return to Roots fever that swept the western world. Ohr *Somayach* became one more source of income for me as I struggled to keep alive what I had built both in the coffee house circuit and on the campus scene. This, too, lasted only a year or so before they realized it had not been profitable for them to sponsor a guy who didn't send potential Root Returners to their yeshiva but to other yeshivot. Basically, I was sending people where I felt they'd fit in, not where I was expected to send them by my sponsors. But by this time, around 1979, I had some freelance editing work to fall back on and was recruited by the late, blessed Jack Goldman, owner of Judaica Press, to write ads and press releases for new books. Little did I know that several of those new books would soon be written by me. The outreach work continued without sponsorship as a private venture between myself and the communities of Massapequa and North Bellmore. I continued my visits to Stony Brook campus as well, continuing my outreach work there out of my already drained pockets.

As a devoted ultra-Orthodox Jew, nothing was going to stand in my way, nothing was going to prevent me from carrying out the will of God: that I bring the wayward Israelites back to their rightful path. Often I brought my work home, inviting unaffiliated young Jews to our Sabbath table for a taste of authentic Judaism. It was a pretty sure way to turn people around, to demonstrate to them that genuine Jewish living is replete with spirituality and meaning, unlike the freeze-dried Judaism with which they'd been reared. But the coffee houses were only half of a solution to half the problem. The other half was aimed at educating parents so that their kids wouldn't get turned off to begin with. The adult education program I started in Massapequa became the preventive measure and it not only educated the grown-ups about the Judaism they never knew, but it also changed their lives and moved them to practice and commitment.

Behind my humble back I had become famous, renowned in the Orthodox community for my hard work and personal and financial sacrifices on behalf of the lost tribes of Israel. I was reeling 'em in. I was turning assimilated Jews, both young and old, into ultra-Orthodox Jews. To do all this I was going into hock, using my own and my father's meager earnings to rent cars, buy books, run weekend retreats, set up outreach tables in Stony Brook, print posters.

Even as the adult ed group began giving me handouts, I was still suffering financial hardships because back home I was raising a family that had mysteriously gone from just me and Bryna to me and Bryna and three young daughters. Rent was high. We needed more space and the rent at the next apartment was even higher than high. Medicine, doctors, vitamins, rent, groceries, clothes ...

> When a man marries, he becomes like a donkey,
> carrying burdens from here to there, and from there
> to here. When he gains a family, he becomes like a
> dog, panting heavily while hurrying from one place
> to the other, unashamedly begging his needs and
> taking them from one place and putting them into
> another place, to and fro, to and fro.
>
> *Midrash Tanchuma, P'kudei*, No. 3

But not to worry. God will provide. And God did provide. Mostly through interest-free loans that I could not afford to repay. I prayed hard and maintained my faith in God's compensation, at least for tips and expenses, but to no avail. With each personal and financial sacrifice, I expected God to reward me richly for all the holy work I was doing in the world. But no response. The Jews-for-Jesus, however, were doing fine.

> Once, Rabbi Akiva and his disciples were strolling
> past a house of idolatry when the disciples noticed a
> lame man going in and shortly thereafter coming out
> healed, then a blind man entered and came out
> cured. Said they: "Master, how could this be?" Said
> he: "God's compassion knows no bounds. Says the
> Compassionate One: 'Should I withhold their healing
> just because their time for healing happens to
> coincide with their visit to the house of idolatry?'"
>
> *Midrash Aseret HaDib'rot*

In 1580, Rabbi Yehudah Loew of Prague chanted some ancient Hebraic mystical incantations and created a Golem, a lump of clay which he then animated into a powerful monster that would protect the Jews of Bohemia from anti-Semitic persecutions. In 1980, exactly four hundred years later, I resurrected the Golem of Prague in an embellished version of the original legend, not to avert persecution but to earn a living. Judaica Press paid me as I wrote in lieu of royalties. With my luck, however, the book took off and remains in print at this writing, a popular book amongst primarily Orthodox Jews across the globe. Those who hadn't known me for my successful outreach work now knew me for my bestseller. Since my paycheck ceased with the completion of the book, I had to write some more books, and write I did as I now became a famous author in the Orthodox Jewish world.

Fame does not necessarily bring fortune. Yet I continued my outreach work at great personal expense and hardship. I was a soldier of God engaged in a holy war, and nothing could stop me now. Nothing. I was now *Rabbi Winkler* the author and outreach worker, newly ordained by the elder dean of the yeshiva back in Jerusalem whose wish for me had finally come true. I had a good reputation. I was honored, respected. People greeted me on the street, knew who I was. I was somebody. Soon I was asked to teach at two different *yeshivot* that catered to non-Orthodox Jewish men seeking to learn about orthodoxy. I was a rabbi, an outreach worker, an author, and now even an official teacher at a *yeshiva*.

My reputation as a teacher rippled across the continent even as far as the West Coast. One day I received a letter from a young Jewish woman in Los Angeles who was being swept into Christianity by the influence of friendly missionaries. She had gotten hold of my name from her aunt's boyfriend's son-in-law's first wife's second cousin's best friend, and she wanted to ask me some questions concerning why it was that Jews didn't believe in Jesus as the Messiah and son of God. I wrote her back. She wrote back, I wrote back, each of us playing ping-pong with scriptural quotes. Finally, I sat down and composed a once-and-for-all, 53-page, single-spaced letter going through each and every proof brought by Christian missionaries down the ages. In a week, the packet came back. She had moved and left no forwarding address. I threw the packet in the trunk of my car, frustrated that I had spent so much time writing that epistle only to get it returned by the postal service.

While I failed at making a living outside of borrowing, I succeeded in interpreting Torah for the contemporary mindset even of the most alienated of my people. I drew young men and women to my classes, ranging from those who were seeking reconnection to their Jewish roots, to those who were otherwise firmly planted in the ashrams of Buddhism and Hinduism. I could speak their lingo, understand their soul yearning, and reach them across any moat.

As for the Evil Inclination, he would often creep up on me and distract my mind while teaching women, introducing fantasies like one day they would all become my wives. I mean, it was ludicrous, he argued, that I should go through this so very short lifetime having tasted love with only one woman. It was unfair, he complained, that God should parade in front of me so many women to whom I felt so deeply attracted—toward what purpose? Did God enjoy teasing me? What, indeed, was the point of all these incredible encounters with all these incredible sirens?

Abraham would teach the men;

Sarah would teach the women.

☙ Midrash B'reishis Rabbah 39:14

The Evil One was right. It made absolutely no sense whatsoever. No doubt they were all meant to be my wives. Every one of them, but especially the single moms, sentenced to years of raising their children singlehandedly and perhaps even longer periods without physical intimacy. Soon I became obsessed with the ancient and medieval textual sources around polygamy, how it was never an issue in Jewish law until the tenth century, and even then only amongst Occidental Jews, not Oriental Jews. When in the tenth century Rabbi Gershom M'or Hagolah did ban polygamy for the European Jewish communities, it had clearly been in response to Church pressure. In the eyes of the Church back then practically everything that Judaism permitted was considered either fornication or satanic. Wisely, however, he had limited his ban to "the end of the fifth millennium," which in the Hebrew reckoning ended well over seven centuries ago. The ban continued nonetheless because Christian animosity against the Jews continued nonetheless. The Jewish communities of the Orient and Africa, however, were not affected by the ban, since the Church had no influence on those parts of the world back then.

My mother once told me that when I was little I asked my father whether he, too, had many wives as did our ancestors.

Then there were these teachings about the alternative to marriage known as *pilag'shut*, literally: "half marriage," which is more commonly known as "living together." These teachings I brought to my classes and introduced as well to single women and men who were dying for sexual intimacy but were not ready to marry. It was not by any means some kind of advocacy or crusade on my part, but a response to the questions that would come up around the issues of premarital sex. The more I listened and took in the anguish communicated to me by single people, the more I voiced the ancient teachings that provided for reasonable options.

It all began quite innocently when I got tired of giving pat party-line responses to real hard, heart questions from those attending my classes. Questions like: "Does this mean I have to stop living with my boyfriend/girlfriend in order to observe the Torah?" And my answer was of course "Yes. That's what it means." I would then return home that evening feeling like a thief, having kept from the seekers alternatives and possibilities for their lives that were fully sanctioned in the Torah. Therefore, I decided to risk everything and tell it like it is. I would simply show them the sources in the original Hebraic and Aramaic texts and let them decide on their own. At first, such individuals would break out in joy over the hope that I had brought them, the gift of option and possibility. But then they turned against me, frightened away by the radicalness of it all, the shock of it all, especially when everything I told them was shot down by the other rabbis in their lives to whom they hurried for confirmation. While at one time deeply thirsty for sexual intimacy, they suddenly felt sated, even terrified by the idea, after I'd shown them that it was permitted.

> The Evil Inclination desires only that which is forbidden. Once, during the fast of Yom Kippur, Rabbi Menna went to visit Rabbi Chaggai who was ill. Said Rabbi Chaggai: "I am so very thirsty." Said Rabbi Menna: "Then break the fast and drink something." An hour later, Rabbi Menna returned and asked: "How is your thirst?" Said Rabbi Chaggai: "No sooner had you permitted me to drink than the desire left me."
>
> ✌ **Jerusalem Talmud, *Yoma* 6:4**

The other rabbis were slowly losing their faith in me as I continued to ignore their demands that I desist from exposing such teachings to the laity. Finally I was asked to leave the yeshiva. I left. And in so doing, I felt a piece of me leaving the party-line stance of my community altogether. Soon, the myriad of lenient religious rulings and dicta that I had been busily recovering for others, I now began recovering for myself. And, mind you, they weren't all about sex. There are many lenient teachings around other laws too, such as the amount of time a Jew waits between eating a meat dish and a dairy dish, or around women wearing prayer shawls and infuencing religious legislation, or around the requirements for conversion, or around the question of electricity on the Sabbath, or around contraception and abortion and lesbianism and Passover restrictions and prayer requirements and sorcery and Sabbath observance, and so on.

Little by little, as I was searching for ways to lighten the rigidity of religious regimen for others, I was also easing it for myself. I had been raised by a particular Orthodox party-line which had until now worked for me, been my Truth and Conviction, and which at this juncture of my life had lost its flavor and immanence. Sort of like your favorite gum. Chew it long enough and eventually you either spit it out altogether or you lovingly store it underneath a desk or chair. For me, it was not a spiteful rejection but an organic mutation; not a deliberate progression but a natural evolution.

I owe everything to the Orthodox tradition in which I was reared and so thoroughly educated and marinated. To this day, I study the very same ancient writ as I did when I was living the Orthodox way; the same books grace my shelves now as then. It was just that a dimension of my Selfhood was ripening at this time of my life and ready to either be hatched into a whole new being, or turned into yet one more breakfast of scrambled eggs with ketchup.

This major shift in my practice and mindset upset Bryna deeply, challenging her unbending devotion to the ways and means of the rabbinate with whom she had long ago embedded her allegiance, and whose rulings she respected as non-negotiable application of Torah law and observance.

As for my fantasies around husbanding multiple wives, they remained just that: fantasies. The Jewish community of the Occident was not ready for the resurrection of the Judaism of the Orient with its extended family structure and its uninhibited sensuality (and neither was Bryna). It was still living the way it had been compelled to live by religious cosmologies otherwise alien to its very core. For me, polygamy and *pilag'shut* were real possibilities, the prudish taboos against which continued to keep a lot of people single, without families of their own, and without families to share. Under the guise of monogamy, men and women of the culture perpetuating these taboos were instead cheating behind each other's backs, or engaged in serial monogamy, meaning marrying and divorcing, marrying and divorcing. And single women joined married folk at their dinner tables secretly burning with painful jealousy over the experience of husband and family that they could not share. And married women were draining their own blood and energy trying to single-handedly raise children numbering anywhere from four to fifteen, when none of their ancestral mothers raised half as many by themselves but shared childrearing with other women members of the family.

My stand on all these issues was of course funded by the Evil Inclination, but the motif was not completely one of salivating lechiness.

Rabbi Me'ir (2nd century) used to mock at those too weak to withstand the Evil Inclination. One day the Evil Inclination appeared to him on the other side of the river in the likeness of a beautiful woman gesturing to him seductively. Seeing that there was no boat, Rabbi Me'ir grabbed hold of a rope and swung across the river, overcome by passion. Half way across, the apparition disappeared and the Evil Inclination reappeared in its place and said to him: "If

the heavenly hosts would not have briefed me, saying
'Beware of Rabbi Me'ir and his Torah,' I would not
have assessed your worth at even two cents."

❧ Babylonian Talmud, *Kidushin* 81a

Meanwhile, I was in deep hock financially, and for some odd reason God was not helping me out in spite of my sincere prayers and good deeds. I was soon to learn why. Had God answered my prayers I would today still be living in New York in a lifestyle that was slowly choking my spirit.

Chapter Six

Exodus

> You don't know what the absolute truth is.
>
> And no one has the right to tell you what it is.
>
> Because it is yours alone to seek and yours alone to discover.
>
> Someone else's truth will always be theirs, not yours. Never yours.
>
> **ﬠ§ The Evil Inclination**

One day it became crystal clear to me that nothing at all was crystal clear to me. Everything that was right and true in my life felt all wrong and false for me. So I packed a lunch and left for Hollywood.

> No man crosses the boundary of what is right
>
> unless he is overcome by a spirit of foolishness.
>
> **ﬠ§ Babylonian Talmud, *Sotah* 3a**

My life was falling apart, the fate of a marriage and three little girls hung in the balance, and I was going to Hollywood to tell jokes. I figured that if I failed to "find myself" maybe I'd at least get a crack at doing stand-up at the Improv. It was somehow obvious to me that if I could teach Talmud and write about Kabbalah, I could certainly do comedy.

I crossed the Verazzano Bridge anticipating a deep sense of relief but experienced instead a deep sense of anguish and an even deeper sense of terror. Off the shiny side of a passing blue van, I noticed the reflection of my car, and then of me inside it, driving. It then hit me that I was a 32-year-old man running away from home. Even better: a famous rabbi running away from home; a successful author with—as my mother still puts it—"such a good reputation," running from certain fame and posterity in search of Fool's Gold. I was, as Dr. Carl Hammerschlag would later diagnose me: a schmuck. In that brief reflection I saw a Jew fleeing, not from hordes of marauding Cossacks or goose-stepping Nazis, but from Brooklyn, from the most dependable safety net and comfort zone ever known to Jewry. I was fleeing everything Judaism stood for: family, community, the Holy Torah, and kosher pizza. And where was I going? For what great and awesome Nirvana was I leaving all this behind?

Naarishkeit. Or, in English: Burbank.

Well, I'm driving 'cross Highway-40 contemplatin' my life;
Only four days ago on the eastern coast
I left my children and my wife;
Goin' all the way out to California
so's I can watch the sun go down;
And get a good grip on my mind before I lose it
and turn my life around.

✌️ Song:1982

Cheap motels, white line fever, fear about not succeeding in my failure to live the way I didn't want to live, doubt about the wisdom of driving another mile farther from familiarity and security to chaos and uncertainty, wonder about what God thought of all this, and—more importantly—whether God approved.

And I was very horny.

> Said Rabbi Elai the Elder (1st century):
> "If a man sees that his lustful inclination is
> getting the best of him, he should go to a place
> where no one knows him,
> cloak himself in anonymity,

ह On mother Esther's lap,
Denmark, 1949, wondering
if being born was really
such a good idea.

ह Gershon (right) trying
to warn skeptical brother
Michael about the Evil One.

〰 Listening to an amusing oration
by the Evil Inclination, circa 1956.

❧ "Innocence" 1967.

❧ En route to the DMZ
in Korea, 1969.

ह≥ **Still Orthodox in the army, 1969.**

ह≥ **Model soldier,**
South Korea, 1970.

ह॰ॐ With colleague Rabbi Yosef Ratzabi, Israel 1979.

ह॰ॐ Co-performing a wedding with Rabbi Shlomo Carlebach (on right) in the Colorado Rockies, 1985.

ৈ❧ Irreverent benediction over bread at a wedding
in West Virginia, 1986.

ৈ❧ Dancing for brother Dov and sister Shoshanah,
Colorado, 1986.

≈ **Resting after a long day of herding sheep,
West Virginia.**

ॐ Ranching in Colorado.

ॐ With daughters Miriam Chara (left)
and Sora Baila, following a wild tagging
spree, Brooklyn, 1989.

ৡৠ Gershon and Lakme's wedding at Mt. Eden
Retreat Center, New Jersey, 1991.

ৡৠ "Ahhh, a taste of heaven." In the woods of
New Mexico.

ক্ষ A newly married couple promises to honor each
other forever if the rabbi will only stop singing,
West Virginia, 1991.

ক্ষ Greeting schmelves
(Jewish elves) while
hiking in the New
Mexico wilderness.

Photo by Tana

↋ A rare photo of author's meeting
with a schmelf (daughter Aharonit), 1996.

Photo by Peter Grotte-Higley

དྷ Driving away the Evil One
on his land in New Mexico.

ह्युष्ट Teaching in the redwoods of Oregon
while supporting a weary tree.

ह्युष्ट Gershon's mother Esther critiquing his
ensemble while his father, Manasse, marvels
at his great-grandchild, Naomi.

ּּ Teaching and levitating in a Bedouin tent
in the Judean Desert, Israel, 1999.

ಶಿ With Palestinian Sheikh Ali Saleh
Muhammed Hussein and his son
Yakoub Hussein, New Mexico, 1999.

ಶಿ Gershon and Lakme with
daughter Aharonit.

ಶ‍ Laughing with God, Missoula,
Montana, 2001.

Exodus

wrap himself in black,

and do what his heart desires,

and let him thereby not profane

the Holy Name in public."

᭣ৡ **Babylonian Talmud,** *Kiddushin* **40a**

I had just taken a leap of faith into total freedom from any religious imperative such as sex only in marriage and only with a Jewess and only between menstrual cycles. And here I was, on the road, far away from the nearest rabbi and the Code of Jewish Law, in the land of the Hittites and Amorites, in a place where no one knew of me and where I would not profane the Holy Name in public—which meant that whatever I did, they wouldn't blame it on the Jews, or—as Rabbi Elai the Elder had meant it: no one would say something like "See that man of God and the evil he has committed? Some God *he's* got!" No. Here on the road I was safe. Here the Holy Name would not meet with defamation. Here, anything went and no one would know but God, who was feeling to me less and less religious with every five hundred miles.

Well, I just passed Albuquerque

but it don't feel far enough;

Gonna have to keep on drivin'

'til I can prove this trip's no bluff;

and I sure miss warm home cookin'

and the comfort of my bed;

but I know I'm just a dreamin'

'cuz back home I was as good as dead.

᭣ৡ **song:1982**

By the time I got to Phoenix I felt this incredible sense of "you can't touch me" freedom that cracked open dams inside of me that I never realized were there. Floods of wanting, lusting, life-ing, poured uncontrollably from my being. Actually, I was having a wet dream at a rest area.

> A man should be ever so careful of his thoughts
> during the day, lest he come to nocturnal
> emission during the night.
>
> ᵉᶜᵍ **Babylonian Talmud,** *Ketubot* **46a**

It became clear to me that I had to stop at the next town and find a woman to sleep with. I needed badly to be cradled in the warm sensuous arms of a woman who wasn't going to think about rabbinic saints while she was making love to me, and who wouldn't care about the covers slip-sliding away from our naked sweaty bodies as we wrestled one another in unrestrained passion; someone with whom I wouldn't have to make love with a flashlight because the room had to be dark.

Godforbid, there was nothing about any of this that was out of the bounds of the Torah. I may have cast off my "party-line" ties with Torah, but my essential roots in Torah were still pretty much in tact. What I lusted for did not in any way deviate from what the patriarch Judah had done some 3,500 years earlier, in spite of what the holy commentators rationalized. Except Judah had gone to town looking for a prostitute (Genesis, Ch. 38) and I was just looking for a woman who would want to bed me. Judah, however, was far more experienced than I was and knew it was more likely that a Sacred Prostitute would willingly bed a stranger than would a blind date. But the fact is that the patriarch Judah had done it, and, as the ancients implored us to ask: "When will my actions compare to those of my ancestors?" (*Midrash Tana D'bei Eliyahu*, Ch. 25). And as Hillel the Elder taught: "If not now, when?" (Babylonian Talmud, *Avot* 2:4). Moreover, since this was going to be my first time, I was determined to do it right, exactly as prescribed in the Torah in the story of Judah. For example, instead of paying cash I was going to leave the woman my hiking stick as collateral, just like Judah had done, and tell her I'd have some sheep delivered to her later, just like Judah did. If this was unacceptable, I would use my father's American Express card.

> While there exists no real prohibition
>
> against a Jewish man making love
>
> with an Aramite woman,
>
> if he does so nonetheless,
>
> zealots are permitted to smite him,
>
> but only during the act,
>
> and only if he commits the act
>
> in front of a Jewish public.

> **❧ Babylonian Talmud, *Sanhedrin* 81b**

I checked into a motel in Yuma, Arizona, and looked up "Prostitutes" in the local Yellow Pages. But first I looked up Zealots—just in case. To my utter dismay, neither was listed. I would have stood a far better chance had I stopped off in Phoenix. They have a much bigger Yellow Pages there, and—as I was to learn much later—"Escort Service" does not imply some sort of a pilot truck, though it does have something to do with oversized loads. So here I was, ready to commit my first transgression, overturn my first taboo, and I'm stuck in a town with no sin.

> Then asked Rabbi Nattan:
>
> "Pray tell, what did God do?"
>
> Replied Elijah:
>
> "The Holy Blessed One laughed."

> **❧ Babylonian Talmud, *Babba Mezia* 59b**

Indeed I imagined God bent over in deep belly laughter, hardly able to catch a cosmic breath: "He ... he ... he was looking through the Yellow Pages ... Ho ho ho hahahahaaaaaaaaaaaaa! ... and ... and ... and just when he's ready to throw all caution to the wind—there's not even a breeze!!! Ho ho ho hahahahaaaaaaaaaaa what a *schmuck*—what a *yold!*"

> A good intention does God consider
> as if it were actually committed.
> An evil intention does God *not* consider
> as if it were actually committed.
>
> **Babylonian Talmud, *Kiddushin* 40a**

Phew!

As I crossed the vast desert of southeastern California, the nudnicking urgings of Fear-Of-The-Unknown, of What-If-This-Is-Wrong, ceased gnawing at me, and were swept away by the desert winds. Now I wanted only to go forward, only forward, and I hadn't even transgressed a single commandment yet. Every cactus along the way threw its arms up and shrugged at me, as if it was admonishing me Jewish-style: "Nu? So you think you're such a hotshot? Such a *yeshivisher* Jimmy Dean driving romantically into the sunset? So you think you're such a wise guy who knows what's best for him? You think you know better than thousands of years of wisdom of what's good for you—of what's right and true? It's not too late, *chelm'nik*, to turn around that poor excuse for a *Merkava* you're driving and get back on the right path.

> So part of me says: "Turn that car around!"
> on account of the young;
> and the other part says: "No way, ol' buddy,
> this song has gotta be sung";
> and the Arizona mountains
> well, they're urging me on,
> and I'm afraid if I so much as hesitate
> my second chance'll be gone.
>
> **song:1982**

I pulled off the road to take a leak. When I stepped out of the car a large raven was waiting beside a sagebush to greet me. He hopped two paces eastward, the direction of Brooklyn and Jerusalem, and then stopped. I recognized him, that hypocritical sonofabitch. It was the very same raven that Noah had dispatched during the Great Flood to scout the earth for any signs that the waters were receding, that the world was ready to start anew. The ancient rabbis explain that the raven had declined the mission, circled the ark, and returned (Genesis 8:7) because he didn't trust Noah alone with his mate (Babylonian Talmud, *Sanhedrin* 108b). Consequently, Noah had to send a less paranoid and more faithful kind of bird, a dove, who ultimately returned with a twig in her beak (Genesis 8:11). But God is a fair judge: the image of the dove carrying a twig in her beak was to become an international symbol of peace and hope, while the raven was to end up a half-assed symbol of horror movies and literary thrillers.

> Rabbi Ilish (3rd century) came upon a raven
> who shrieked at him to warn him of danger:
> "Ilish run away! Ilish run away!"
> He paid no mind to it. Later, a dove
> appeared to him and issued the same
> warning and he listened to it and fled.
>
> **Babylonian Talmud, *Gittin* 45a**

But then there were the ravens who fed Elijah the Prophet when he went into hiding (I Kings 17:6). So they could be good omens, too, provided you were hiding out in a dark cold cave after telling off the king.

"So what have you been sent to tell me, O raven?" I asked as the raven flew a couple of yards up on a fence post. "That I should turn back? That I've made the wrong decision? That this is not the way? That the life I was living so devoutly before is the right way, the true way, the only way for a Jew to live?"

The raven held its head aloof, as if it was saying: "What—is he talking to me? What a *schmeggeg*. What a *schmeggeg*."

The raven's response sent shudders up my spine and across every rib, then down again and out my tailbone. Then it hit me. The raven had not been sent to tell me anything. It had been sent to show me what I would become if I didn't turn back immediately. I would become the raven. I would become someone who left the ark only to fly in circles and then return. It was a prophecy, I surmised, a prophecy I didn't want to face. The raven, satisfied I'd gotten the message, took off and flew west, the direction I was heading. This confused me, so I looked around for a dove.

If indeed I was to return, it had to be soon, because I was actually getting closer and closer to that terrifying point of no return. And what about God? What about the Creator of the beautiful red mesa towering before me against the royal blue sky? What about the divinity I had been so faithfully worshiping since childhood, and for whom I got left back in Army Basic Training again and again? What about being true to the God I believed in? What if the Orthodox path was the right one after all, as it had felt so authentically and deeply for me during thirty-two years of my life, physically, emotionally, intellectually, and spiritually? If it had been truth for me all these years, how could it not be truth for me now? It was not too late to turn back, to confess my wrongness and return to the God of Brooklyn.

> The Holy Blessed One follows the sinner patiently
> through the marketplace, ready at every moment
> to receive them back in penance.
>
> **Midrash Pesik'ta D'Rav Kahana 146b**

I climbed the fence and ran up the rocky slope to a cleft in the rock and waited there for an answer, just like Moses did when he asked to see the divine glory (Exodus 33:21). Nothing happened. All I heard was a breeze sweeping up the other side of the ridge, and a distant tractor trailer shifting into lower gear on the highway below. Maybe God wasn't going to pass over the opening of the cleft in the rock. Maybe, I wondered, maybe, I felt, maybe God was already in the cleft itself, right behind me, breathing down the back of my neck, following me through the marketplace patiently waiting for the moment when I would decide I'd had enough and wanted to come home.

I turned around.

"I want to be true to you," I declared to the sandstone wall behind me. "But I cannot be true to you if I am untrue to myself. Therefore, even if the authentic path one ought to walk in order to be true to you is the very path from which I have just strayed, still I cannot go back to it because on that path I no longer feel true to myself. And if I cannot be true to myself, then neither can I feel true to You. In other words, what I'm trying to say is ..."

I was interrupted by the sound of movement in the brush below. I leaned over the edge of the cleft to get a closer look at God's reply. It was a stray dog taking a crap.

And the Word of God came to me saying: "Son of a gun, thy prayer and theological grapplings are intriguing unto Me. I have heard thy supplications and have beheld thy plight. But lo! thine bladder is full and thy body writhes in discomfort. Take heed of the dog who sees to its needs, for the path that leads one to pee when the bladder is full, or to poop when the bowel is abundant, is more dear to Me than any other path. Pay heed, then, to the care-free dog below, who has indeed discovered Ultimate Truth in the moment and for herself. Observe, too, how she has stepped off the path to enjoy her discovery. Know, then, that she will again step on and off numerous paths in her journey, paying heed not to which path she is on or to whether a path is there altogether, but paying heed only to the journey, only to the journey."

Explained Rabbah (3rd century):
"I am weary of Rabbi Hisda's discourses,

for he teaches only of mundane matters.
Like, when one is taking a crap,
one should not force the bowel movement,
and like what kinds of material one should
and should not use to wipe oneself."
Said Rabbi Huna to him: "All the more reason why
you SHOULD study with him. For he occupies himself with
the workings of God's creations. And you call that mundane?"

≈§ Babylonian Talmud, *Shabbat* 82a

I took a leak.

During the next several hours on the road I began to feel the
onset of sensations of relief which felt as real and as powerful as
the sensations of regret I had experienced during the first three days
of the journey. Now, the farther I drove the lighter I felt, the more
right the trip felt, my leaving, my shifting—in spite of the fact that
I had no idea where I was going or what I was going to do when
I got there.

So, good-bye, New York City,
hello, desert and rock;
I just broke through my chains,
now it's time to throw away the lock;
I'm free to roam and wander,
gonna drive right through eternity;
gonna do all the things I've been longin' to do
like gettin' back in touch with me.

≈§ song:1982

Needless to say, freedom and the lightness of being can be costly.
This realization dampened my sense of rightness about what I was
doing. Face it, as romantic as all this was becoming, pretty soon I'd
be running out of money. Then I'd be running out of gas. Then food.

Then lodging. Then hope. Before I knew it I would probably have to call my father rather than take money from the wife and kids, and the conversation would most likely go something like this:

———————

"Hello, Far?" [Far is Danish for father: spelled fader]

"Hello, Gersheleh, mine *zeeseh kihnd* [*Yiddish:* my sweet child]. What's doing?"

"Oh, nothing much."

"Where are you calling from?"

"Uh ... Needles."

"Needles?"

"Needles."

"And where is Needles? New Jersey?"

"No, it's in California."

"Is there a shul there?"

"I don't think so."

"Are there Jews there?"

"I don't see any."

"You know who I met today on the subway?"

"Uh uh."

"I met a young man who said he knew you."

"Oh?"

"I think his name is Franken, or Frankel, maybe Freinkel, or maybe it was Gutman, or something like that. He knew you when you were teaching at the yeshiva."

"Oh yeah, I think I know who you mean."

"He said he was very grateful to you for making him *frum.* You helped him to become Orthodox when he was about to give up. He said you succeeded in talking him out of Buddhism ... "

"Oy, God forgive me ... Listen, Far, I need to ask you if you can wire me some ... "

"Oh, you know who else has been asking about you? Remember Rabbi Hirschman? He was your *rebbe* in *yeshiva* when you were in third grade ... "

My mother would then get on the other phone and interrupt:

"'Nash, who are you talking to? Is that Gershon? Gershon is that you? 'Nash, why didn't you tell me it was Gershon? So where are you?"

"Needles."

"Needles? Er han hil tzossel? [*Danish:* Is he completely mad?] Where are you really?"

"Needles."

"*Noch ah mohl mit dem shpulkas* [*Yiddish:* Again with the needles]— *val er dog i vein med ham* [*Danish:* What is wrong with him]? Why won't you tell us where you are?

"California!"

"So why didn't you say so?"

"Needles is a place in California."

"And your place is in Brooklyn. How could you do this? What about the children? At least have *rachmonus* [*Hebrew:* compassion] on them. How could you leave just like that?"

"It wasn't 'just like that.' It had been building up for over a year."

"Tell that to the children."

"I did. I explained things to them. I told them that if I stayed they would have a father who was sad, and if I left they would have a father who was happy, and that it had nothing to do with them. And I write to them every day from the road. I care about them."

"You care about them? That's why you left them?"

"I didn't leave them. I'll be back soon. I just need to get away from everybody and everything so I could think. I just need to be somewhere where I can have the peace and the distance to figure things out."

"What's wrong with Staten Island?"

"I can think better out here."

"In Needles you can think better? Maybe it's *takkeh* what you need, *ah gut gezunteh shtek mit'n shpulkeh* [*Yiddish:* a good, healthy stab with a needle]. Maybe it would wake you up. How could you just go away and leave behind such a wonderful wife and three young children? This isn't the Gershon we know. And what is it that you need to think about and figure out? You have such a good reputation! You're a respected rabbi and a famous author. Everybody knows your name. Everybody has your books."

"In Needles they don't have my books and they don't know my name."

"So why are you there?"

"I need to be anonymous."

"So come back! We won't tell anyone you're here. You can wear a shopping bag over your head. I don't understand. What has happened to you? Everybody thinks the world of you here. You have a family here, and you've built a good name for yourself. What more do you want?"

"I want to find out who I am outside of my reputation, outside of my books, outside of everyone else's idea of who I am and ought to be, so I can find out who I am becoming. Because deep inside I am feeling that I am becoming something other than who I have been. There's change going on in me, important change, and I need to find some fresh soil in which to plant it and nurture it. It's like I feel there's an important existential shift happening and I don't want to be left back again like in Basic Training."

"*Vos retts du ah zoy fil naarishkeit* [*Yiddish:* Why are you speaking so much nonsense]? 'Nash, say something to him! He's your son!"

My father would then clear his throat and speak, ever so softly and non-judgmentally:

"Gersheleh."

"Yes, father."

"Did you know Mister Kleinholtz?"

"With the really bad limp?"

"That's right. But he's not limping anymore."

"Oh? They finally operated?"

"No, he died."

"'Nash!!!'"

Chapter Seven

The Sexual Revelation

Said Rabbi Shim'on (3rd century):
"The sexual urges of men are far
more intense that those of women."
Asked Rabbi Yochanan: "What proof do you bring?"
Replied Rabbi Shim'on: "Look into the marketplace
and notice who is looking for whom."

Babylonian Talmud, *Ketuvot* 64b

Anyone who has ever driven to Los Angeles knows that you never actually get there, because there are no indications of when you have arrived. It is a city with no beginning, no middle, and no end. It begins east of San Bernardino, some 90 miles away, and ends somewhere along the outer rim of the Solar System. When I first drove through it in that momentous summer of 1982, I just kept driving because I had no idea of where to exit. But my initial feeling about L.A. was this rush of excitement that swept through my being, triggered by the sight of tropical trees along the highway, scenic hills to the north, and the illusion of hope and promise impregnated by the stereotypical image of L.A. as the place where dreams get developed—sort of like a cosmic Fotomat. Here, I thought, was where my yet undefined dreams would take form and flourish. Here, I thought, whatever needed to happen next in my life would take root and blossom. Here, I thought, whatever personal change was going on inside of me would become clear to me, and so would whatever "next step" I needed to take for myself, spiritually and emotionally.

But first I needed to drum up some replenishment for my rapidly dwindling monetary resources. Not to worry, I thought to myself as I eyed the exit for Burbank: Hollywood here I come. I would become a screenwriter in no time, especially with four published books to my name. Of course the books were about Jewish folklore and mysticism and some esoteric Judaic philosophy, but what difference would it make to Warner Brothers whether I'd written a book about the five levels of the soul or *The Pelican Brief?* A writer is a writer! Finished.

I checked into an All American motel run by a family of Hindus from Bombay who spoke barely enough English to register me. I must have given them the impression that I was some important Hollywood writer because they treated me like royalty, or perhaps they saw clear through my karmic mess and pitied me in my journey. I was, after all, reincarnating in a single lifetime. I had died a perspiring rabbi and was coming back an aspiring screenwriter.

> Said Rav (3rd century): "The Evil Inclination
> first appears to you like a distant wayfarer.
> Then he becomes as a guest in your home.
> And before you realize it, he becomes your master."
>
> **◄§ Babylonian Talmud, *Sukah* 52b**

But now that I was settled in what I believed was my destination, the Evil Inclination resumed its program of trying to get me laid. I had about a hundred bucks in cash, so I hopped in the car and headed for the infamous avenue of sin: Sunset Boulevard. Along the way I crossed Hollywood Boulevard which appeared even more saturated with sin than Sunset, so I parked and strolled by the rows and rows of women of all sizes, shapes, and colors. I was new at this and had no idea of where to begin or how much it would cost.

"Hi, looking for some action?"

I turned around to face a woman so heavily made up I momentarily mistook her for a mannequin.

The Sexual Revelation

"How much does it cost?" I asked naively, assuming this whole *gescheft* was like buying pickles in the Lower East Side. The woman's wig shifted a little as she eyed me suspiciously.

"You a cop?" she asked, straightening her wig. She was slightly taller than me and appeared more aggressive and overbearing than I would have preferred. But I didn't feel it appropriate to walk away from her and leave her feeling rejected or in any way embarrassed.

> It is far better to throw
> oneself into a flaming furnace
> than to embarrass someone in public.
>
> **ᴥ᷎ Babylonian Talmud, *Berakhot* 43b**

I was so concerned about her feelings that I resolved right then and there to make do with her if she was affordable, or leap head first into the nearest pizza oven. I needed a warm feminine body and nothing more complicated than that. With her I may not experience the feminine, but the warmth might be there if she was at all mortal. Indeed, with all that make-up she had on there was no telling what was beneath it all, a She or an It. And night had fallen, so it was too dark to tell.

> When walking alone on the road at night,
> one should not exchange greetings with anyone
> lest they turn out to be a demon.
>
> **ᴥ᷎ Babylonian Talmud, *Megilah* 3a**

I gazed down at her high heels to see whether her feet were bird-like.

"No, I'm not a cop," I said.

"What are you looking for?"

"I just want to sleep with someone. You know, make love."

"How much were you thinking of spending?"

"I don't know. Twenty-five, thirty-five."

"Shit, man, it's gonna cost you about a hundred, at least."

"Nothing for less than that?"

"I can give you a blow job for twenty."

"What's a blow job?"

"Shit, man, you for real?"

I got the feeling that maybe we weren't such a good match after all, and that she wasn't going to fall apart if I were to say Good Night and leave. As I walked off I realized I would probably never have gotten an erection anyway with her, or "it." And a hundred dollars was about all I had left to my name. And to spend a hundred dollars for an orgasm just didn't seem worth it. I would be left broke and spent, with nothing to show for my last dollar but temporary relief from an urge that would shortly thereafter flare up once again, and then again and again.

I continued cruising Hollywood Boulevard unaware that prostitution was legal only in the movies and then only in certain westerns. But though I interviewed at least six prostitutes in the glaring street lights of the busiest boulevard in Los Angeles, I lucked out and was not approached by a single cop.

God watches over the naive.

✺ Psalms 116:6

I decided to drive further away from the Hollywood area. Maybe the high cost of fucking here had to do with location. This was Hollywood. Rich people lived around here. *Schmeggegs* with no future were better off further down the boulevard toward the downtown area. Rabbis who didn't know what a blow job was would perhaps fare better in the less discriminating red light districts of the city of angels. Sure enough, about a mile east of Hollywood I discovered a team of prostitutes huddled in the shadows of a sleazy looking tavern. I was determined. I had to get laid. It was for my health and emotional well-being, I rationalized. God would provide me with a hooker because of my noble intention, my earnest wish to nurture this horny body that belonged to the Almighty, and the distressed soul trapped helplessly inside it.

> More dear to God is a sin committed
> with pure intention than a sacred deed
> performed without pure intention.
>
> **Babylonian Talmud, *Nazir* 23b**

I pulled up to the curb where the women were gathered and one of them approached the car. She seemed nervous and kept looking over her shoulders to spot cops before they spotted her. She stuck her head through the car window and asked me if I was looking for a good time. I quickly checked my Hebrew calendar to make sure this wasn't a fast day commemorating the destruction of the Holy Temple, and said yes, I was. She said she had a friend who could do me for cheap, depending on what I wanted. Thousands of bearded faces enwrapped with prayer shawls flashed before my eyes. It was a glimpse of centuries of holy rabbis watching me from Heaven, wondering what in the hell I was doing.

> When Joseph was being seduced
> by the wife of Potifar, the image of
> his father, Jacob, appeared before him,
> and he did not succumb.
>
> **Babylonian Talmud, *Sotah* 36b**

"You Okay, mister?"

"Yeah, just something in my eye: a patriarch or something."

"A *what?*"

"Never mind. You'd never understand unless you went to a *yeshiva*."

"A *what?*"

"Forget it. Don't mind me, I'm just mumbling."

"Jeez', well, anyway, you want my friend to come over and talk to you?"

"Okay."

Her friend came over, an attractive young black woman with no make-up. She looked completely mortal, warm, feminine. She got in the car, yanked open the glove compartment, and examined it carefully.

"You're not a cop, are you?"

"No. Why is it everyone thinks I'm a cop?"

"We have to be careful. The cops are all over and they're leaning on us hard."

"Why? Is it illegal?"

"Yeah, it's illegal! Where you from, man? You didn't know it was illegal?"

"No. It's my first time. But now I understand why I haven't gotten arrested. Everyone thinks I'm a cop."

"Okay, listen, I'm in a hurry. What are you looking for, honey?"

"I just want to make love."

"You mean all the way?"

"Yeah. I mean, I don't want to get married or anything, just ..."

"You don't want like just a quick blow job?"

"What's a blow job?"

"OK, listen. I can use my friend's room at this motel down the street but we only got like fifteen minutes, so let's go."

"Fifeen minutes? That's pretty short," I protested as I started the car.

"Well, it's gonna have to be a quickie."

"What's a quickie?"

I had hoped for a little bit of intimate conversation followed by some leisurely foreplay, maybe a couple of jokes and a few minutes of sharing and clearing. It would perhaps have gone something like this:

"I want you to know that this is a first for me, and the last thing I want is for you to feel in any way used."

"That is the sweetest thing I've ever heard from a John. But you shouldn't feel like you're using me for the gratification of your sexual urges because that's what I enjoy doing, and especially for someone as nice as you."

"Well, I guess it'd be Okay then, since it's something you enjoy doing anyway. But for me it feels like I'd want to make you feel good, too, as it *should* be in lovemaking of *any* sort, in addition to the money, as the Talmud says: 'A man should never have sex with a woman without first engaging her in foreplay so that her mind will be in harmony with his'" (Babylonian Talmud, *Eruvin* 100b).

"Wow. You're too good to be true. I feel that you are a sensitive, deeply conscientious man, not to mention a prolific talmudic scholar. In fact, you're the first John I've ever met that I've felt drawn to romantically. I feel that I want to make love with you and that I do not want any of your money. I think I value more the quality of friendship and knowing that I sense from you and with you."

"Could I ask you something?"

"Sure. *You* can ask me anything. *Anything.*"

"What's a John?"

But of course it didn't happen that way. Instead I found myself speeding down a dark street off Hollywood Boulevard toward a decrepit looking motel with a prostitute who was in a hurry because her friend was going to need the room for her own clientele at any moment. And there wasn't a moment to lose. I would have to somehow achieve an orgasm before achieving an erection.

After I parked the car, she rushed me through a courtyard full of loitering pimps who threw me knowing glances as I breezed by. Upstairs, the room was bare with only a narrow bed, a chair, and a bathroom. She undressed hurriedly and headed for the bathroom while I fumbled with buttons and zippers, growing nervous and feeling feverish. When she returned she handed me a condom and urged me to hurry up and put it on. She then proceeded to the bed and lay herself flat on her back. While I struggled with the condom—

having never before used one—she went on and on about how we had to hurry because her friend was going to need the room any minute and we had to be out of there in ten minutes. Time was going by and I still couldn't get the condom on because I was completely limp. I lay down alongside her and explained to her that I needed to touch her body first in order to get hard in order to apply the condom. But she grew tense about her friend needing the room at any moment and again repeated the mantra of how we really had to hurry and that she'd really appreciate it if I could cough up forty five bucks instead of thirty six because of the extra hassle she had to go through to get this room. I tried to not hear her rantings and to concentrate instead on the sensations of touching her naked body so that I might get erect and then be able to slip on the condom— but to no avail. I remained limp, she remained tense, I grew anxious, she grew impatient.

Finally, I put the condom on the chair beside the bed and asked her if it would be okay to just not go inside. She said okay but hurry. I swam the sea of femininity that lay before me, wishing so much for her to hold my confusions, soothe my fears, cradle my uncertainties, embrace my loneliness, caress my body, love me, and allow me to kiss her lips. But none of that was forthcoming. I thrust and swayed and wrestled over her body, feeling solitary and lustful, until I came. She jumped out of the bed, grabbed her clothes and disappeared into the bathroom to wash my desperation and neediness from her skin. I dressed, gave her thirty-six dollars and we both headed outside and through the courtyard past a gauntlet of jeering pimps ("Hey, man, she's good, isn't she?") and into my car. I drove her back to her friends, dropped her off with a polite thank you and good night, and bee-lined it back to my Burbank motel, thirty six dollars poorer, no happier for it, and deeply depressed. The rabbis were right. On all counts they were right. Everything the Talmud said was right. I felt ashamed and stupid. I should have known better. I had finally gone and done it and it hadn't been worth the time and energy and gas and cash and frustration. It was, to quote an ancient saying: "Yech p'tooey, feh!" And it cost me thirty six bucks, or twice eighteen, which is the numerical equivalent for the Hebrew word for Live—(*chai*). A good omen but a bad lay.

It was said of Rabbi El'azar the son of Dordayo (2nd century) that there was not a prostitute anywhere with whom he had not already slept. One day he heard about a prostitute who lived far across many rivers and who demanded a purse full of *dinarim* from anyone who wished to lay with her. Rabbi El'azar took a purse full of *dinarim* and journeyed across seven rivers until he arrived at her mansion. They were about to make love when she farted. Said she: "Just as this fart will never return to its place of origin, so shall the return (repentance) of Rabbi El'azar the son of Dordayo never be accepted." He went and wept between two mountains until his soul departed. A Heavenly Voice then proclaimed: "Rabbi El'azar the son of Dordayo has achieved his station in the World to Come."

꿯 Babylonian Talmud, Avodah Zarah 17a

Chapter Eight

God the Clown

Rabbi B'ruka of Huza (4th century) and [the ghost of]
Elijah the Prophet were once strolling through a village.
Said the rabbi: "I challenge you to point out anyone in
this entire place who will merit as lofty a position in the
World to Come as will I." Elijah looked about and then
pointed at two men in the distance. Rabbi B'ruka ran over
to them and asked them what holy deeds they had done.
The men looked baffled and replied: "We have done
nothing special. We are just a couple of clowns. When we
see someone who is sad, we make them laugh."

◈ Babylonian Talmud, *Ta'anit* 22a

Having satisfied not my own yearnings but those of the Evil One,
I decided the following day to forego the opportunity of sinning
just because I had become a free man and to instead concentrate
on becoming a successful multi-millionaire comedian and screenwriter. I had a family to support back in New York, I realized, so
this was no time for jerking off, let alone paying for it. My capital was
down to sixty-four dollars. It was time to take action, to realize
hopes, to take yet another of a series of "first steps" into the
unknown. Yesterday I was teaching the Holy Torah in a Brooklyn
yeshiva. Today I was going to cruise the streets of Burbank in the
hope of writing a movie.

I smiled as I drove by studio compound after studio compound
and billboard after billboard portraying the latest in Hollywood

productions. Soon my own movies would be up there: "Invasion of the Velveteen Rabbis"—"Return of the Five Levels of the Soul"—"Night of the Babylonian Talmud II"—"Lost On Hollywood Boulevard"—"The Kleinholtz Limp"—"Condom III"—"The Schmuck."

But instead of becoming a screenwriter I became a comedian. I made many people laugh all across Burbank, especially the doormen at the studio offices and the secretaries of numerous film moguls. Wherever I went looking for work as a writer for television or film, people roared. I was a hit. If anything, I earned points in Heaven for making so many people laugh at me behind my back for thinking I could just walk into a studio and become a writer.

Points in the hereafter, however, don't help much in the here-and-now. I was getting low on cash, and as the third-century Rabbi Chanina put it when he was suffering from a debilitating illness: "I don't need this and I don't need its heavenly reward either" (Babylonian Talmud, *Berachot* 5a). It was becoming more than a cash flow problem, because if it wasn't going to work out here I would have to admit defeat and return to Brooklyn—it would surely be a sign from the Creator that my quest had been a foolish one and that I was to remain on the path I had walked before and that was that. Nor could I go on much longer draining my father's credit card on motel lodging. I had exceeded all limits. I had crossed the boundary. I had shot my credit rating and almost destroyed my father's at the same time. I was getting desperate. It was time to go to West Hollywood and do the Open Mike thing at the Improv and at the Comedy Store. I would get recognized. I would get paying gigs. I would be rich and famous and be able to pay back my father and send lots and lots of money to Bryna and kids and still have enough money left over to rent an efficiency in the hills above Hollywood.

With my dwindling stash I paid the cover charge night after night at The Comedy Store, then at The Improv, observing pathetic wannabees climb up on stage and make complete fools of themselves and bomb. I felt sorry for them. One after another they bombed. I admired Bud Friedman for patiently observing all these *schmeggegs* and giving them the opportunity to try, but they weren't comedians. I'd get up there and show them what comedy was all about. Only I needed an act. So I went back to the motel and worked up an act. It didn't take much to think up something funny to say for three minutes. I mean, I had made my mother and father laugh hundreds of times. I had made people laugh in the army, in the yeshiva, in the street. I had what it took, and Bud Friedman would single me out after my debut and raise me to heights I hadn't dreamed of.

My delivery sucked. My material stunk. But I must have looked a little cute up there—or perhaps pathetic—because I heard a few people laughing somewhere out there amid the great faceless inebriated beyond, rendered invisible by the bright lamps of the stage lights. Later that night, I tried my routine at The Comedy Store, too, and a few people (six to eight people at least) laughed but no talent scout leaped up on stage to give me her card. My act there was followed by this screaming guy who turned everyone off but me. I sat in the audience listening to him talk about his relationship with his girlfriend or with his ex or with life in general, and then he would break out suddenly in curdling screams, usually while his face was virtually pressed against the face of someone seated smack in front of the stage. His anger and frustration found empathy in mine and we met across the dimly lit smoky room, as people up and left in disgust. He thanked me for staying even as the room emptied and I was left alone to be yelled at by the madman. The audience didn't get him. They didn't appreciate his tragi-comedy nor his psychotic-like delivery. I did. For me it was therapeutic, cathartic. He was an escaped minister; I was an escaped rabbi. He and I were brothers in hell. And though I knew then that he would of course never make it as a comic, I nonetheless appreciated the wild, perspiring, screaming, no-holds-barred comedy of Sam Kinnison.

In the end, of course, he became a big hit, screaming his way to stardom and then dying in an automobile accident. I was still alive, but who's to say which is better: a dead successful comic or a live hapless one?

One night, I was sitting in the audience of The Comedy Store when Yaakov Smirnoff stepped up on the stage and did the routine he did for us at the coffeehouse in New York only two years earlier. He wasn't a star yet, but well on his way. I approached him afterward. He remembered me; we talked. But I couldn't hint to him about my situation because he wasn't driving his own Mercedes yet. I wished him luck after his performance and returned to Burbank to spend my last night in a motel.

Nothing had worked out. I wasn't going to make it as a stand-up. Money was down to the last few nickels and dimes. I had all but forgotten the reason I was here to begin with: to re-evaluate my life, my beliefs, my theology, my marriage, my future. Now, the only thing on my mind was survival. Tomorrow I would have to live out of my car and start fasting.

The following day I bid my motel hosts farewell and set off across the hills of Hollywood toward Fairfax, where the nucleus of L.A.'s Orthodox Jewish community was located. I didn't quite go all the way, only toward. There was no way I was going to return to what it was I was seeking distance from. But if a miracle didn't happen soon, I would be left with little choice but to return to the community I'd left—West Coast branch—and surrender myself for a meal and a handout. That's one thing about family. You can always go back to your family and get what you need. Of course it can cost a hefty chunk of guilt, and compromise in areas you might least wish to compromise, but when you're desperate for food and shelter, there's no place like home. Brooklyn was following me and now it had caught up with me and was lurking only inches from where I hid.

I roamed the streets of Hollywood all that day, hoping and dreaming that something would happen to change my situation. I regretted having spent thirty-six bucks on an orgasm but also realized that it would have bought me only one more day of the inevitable. Here I was, down and out in Beverly Hills, wandering the streets, observing people who had homes to go to, people to love, food to eat, cars with fuel, and jobs. Then it hit me. I, too, had a home to go to, people to love and everything else I was hungry for. It was back east in Brooklyn. There, a devoted woman was waiting anxiously to take me back into her arms and into her home. There, three young girls were ready to surround me with hugs and affectionate cuddling. There, was everything I needed. It would be so easy. It would take but one phone call and money would be wired and I could come home, repent, shrug it all off as some premature mid-life crisis, and simply ease right back into the very same saddle I had ridden for years. I'd be back teaching non-Orthodox Jews to become Orthodox. I'd be back running coffee houses for alienated Jewish youth on Long Island. I'd be back bible-babbling with Christian evangelicals on campuses and rescuing unassuming Jewish students from the clutches of their crusades. I'd be back writing books on Jewish mysticism, inspiring assimilating Jews to come home. I could even add a whole new dimension to my outreach work to the unaffiliated among my people: I left the path, saw the folly of leaving, and returned home. Wow. That would inspire even more people to listen to my teachings because I'd have actually been where they had been and tasted of the same forbidden fruit.

With each day of wandering and hoping and not eating, and sleeping in a car with a buck's worth of fuel in the tank, the nagging possibility that my journey was in error grew more and more intense. I called home collect, not to ask for money, but to hear the voices of familiarity, of my wife, of my kids. They missed me. They were worried about me. And I told them that I missed them, too. That I missed home. But I was careful not to let on that I was starving, walking aimlessly about, and sleeping in my car. I wanted to give in and tell them I was wrong about this trip and that I was coming home. But something stopped me. It was that part of me that did not live by bread alone. It was my Evil Inclination, the culprit deep inside of me that had gotten me into this mess to begin with by stirring within me the realization that I wasn't doing life like I really needed life to be for me; that I was living someone else's life, and following someone else's reality map. Would I re-submit to what felt inauthentic to me just because I was hungry and my neck ached from sleeping in my car? Many others before me had gone through far more painful deprivations than these in their quest for personal truth. And I was going to cave in because my car was almost out of gas and I had no money for food and lodging? Picky picky picky.

No. It was not yet time to give up. Fruit and vegetable stores threw out scraps at the end of the day. I nibbled on what I could find that looked Okay. I drank from water fountains at the mall. I didn't need to shave because I sported a beard. I could get away without showering because I still had some deodorant left. In desperation, I walked to The Comedy Store to find Yaakov Smirnoff. I had been instrumental in giving him *his* first break, maybe he would in turn give me *mine*, or at least a couple of bucks for a pastrami sandwich. But he was out of town on a gig. I scanned the want ads of newspapers left on park benches and tried applying for work here and there, as an ice cream vendor, a bull-semen extractor, an actor for a cable-TV network. "We'll call you … By the way, where can we reach you?"

Nowhere. I was unreachable. I was not home. In my search for myself I was losing myself. It was becoming clearer to me that this quest was not what God wanted. Rather, God wanted me back in Brooklyn wrapped in a prayer shawl and phylacteries, swaying back and forth in fervent prayer and thinking holy thoughts. I walked into the La Brea Tar Pits park, sat under a tree and stared at the artificial reconstruction of a mastodon sinking into prehistoric tar en-route to fossilization. I, too, was sinking. So I prayed for some kind of clue, some kind of clarity.

I dozed off, the image of the sinking mastodon and the words of my prayer dancing inside my eyes. Then the Hebrew alphabet appeared and slowly began forming a narrative from the Torah, from the Book of Genesis, from the story of the first Jew, Abraham. It was about how my ancestor had picked up and left what no longer felt right for him and how he had journeyed deep into the wilderness, deep into the uncertain and the unfamiliar, leaving behind everything he had ever known. The voice that had driven him was experienced as the voice of the Creator, who told him: "Go to your self, away from your land, and from your birthplace, and from the house of your parents—to the land that I will show you (Genesis 12:1)."

I awoke with a startle. It was night. Darkness had fallen. The mastodon still hadn't sunk. It only appeared to be sinking. Maybe I, too, was not sinking but only appeared to be. And then it hit me: Abraham had followed the voice blindly. He had not been informed about where he was going, how long it would take for him to get there, or whether the place had a deli. He just up and went because it was something he had to do. And sure enough, when he got "to the land that I will show you" there was nothing to eat and he had to wander off to find food in Egypt, a replica culture of the very kind he had just left behind! But his love of the Creator and the burning sense of his own rightness kept him going. He didn't go back to Brooklyn. He stayed on and stuff began to work out.

Abraham had to interrupt his quest and his settling down in the Promised Land with a temporal side trip to the Egyptian version of the homeland he had left behind. I realized then that to sidetrack to Fairfax proper to get twenty bucks and a corned beef sandwich on rye would not necessarily contradict my quest.

I went back to my car, slept off the remainder of what should have been the dark night of my soul, and dreamed about gefilte fish in jelled broth.

The next morning I started my car on my last few drops of fuel and drove sparingly through Fairfax past hundreds of Jews who still lived the way I used to live, the way I used to convince others to live, the way I once thought was the only way for a Jew to live, the way I no longer felt worked for me. I parked the car up a side street where it could sit for a few days without getting ticketed or towed, and commenced the embarrassing journey to Fairfax Avenue to ask for a handout.

The phone book had listed a Chabad storefront somewhere along the busy stretch of shoppers and wanderers, and I knew that in spite of my theological conflicts with Chabad Hasidism, it was *the* place to go if you were in need. Not that a starving street person wouldn't find a helping hand at any of the synagogues in town, but Chabad folks were hell-bent on making you a good Jew, or making a good Jew an even better one, and those in need knew all too well that for a few minutes of humoring the Chabadniks and letting them show you how to put on *tefillin* or to light the Sabbath candles, you could come away with a full stomach, a couple of bucks, and a place to sleep.

I found the Chabad storefront in no time and walked into what doubled as a Jewish bookstore. A thin, heavily bearded man with a black hat and gold-rimmed glasses approached me instantly and gave me his hand. Since I was starving, my first instinct was to recite a blessing and bite into it, but it didn't seem to have much flesh on it, so I restrained my cannibalistic urges and shook it instead.

"*Sholom aleichem!*" he greeted me heartily. I returned the greeting, "*Aleichem sholom.*"

"Welcome to our store. Feel free to browse around. Did you put on *tefillin* today?"

"Yes," I lied. I needed beef, not leather. I hesitated. I wanted to ask him if he could give me a couple of dollars for a sandwich, but I couldn't bring myself to do it. Pride. What pride? He didn't know who I was. I could just as well have been one more of so many street people, like maybe some guy who grew up in mental institutions and had been released due to overcrowding or lack of funding and now roamed the streets living off of handouts and the goodwill of neighborhood Chabad houses. So what was the big deal?

"What's your name?" he asked, noticing that I wasn't moving or breathing or browsing. I just stood there wondering what I was doing within four cubits of a Hasid when I had just driven 3,000 miles to get away from the very sort of orthodoxy he represented. And I was going to beg him for handout, yet. God, I realized then, has a very strange sense of humor.

"Gershon," I answered, hoping I didn't spoil God's entertainment by not divulging my full name and perhaps getting recognized as *the* Gershon as in Gershon Winkler the famous author and outreach rabbi.

"You're not *the* Gershon, are you?" he asked, "as in Gershon Winkler the famous author and outreach rabbi?"

> The One who dwells
> in the Heavens is laughing.
>
> **Psalms 2:4**

I nodded and he shook my hand again and then pointed proudly to the shelf behind where I was standing, where he displayed a large collection of copies of all my books. Now it was going to be that much harder for me to ask for the handout. Gershon Winkler the famous author and rabbi stranded and hungry in L.A.? How did such a thing come to be? I couldn't bring myself to beg. But I had to and needed to and it would be the most embarrassing thing that I would ever have to do. Where the hell was God? On intermission break? The performance was hardly finished!

Just then, before I could maneuver my lips to form the words "I am hungry and I need food," an angel walked in. God hadn't gone out for popcorn after all. Later on I would recognize this angel: it was the same one that had arrived just in the nick of time to prevent Abraham from sacrificing his son Isaac. She was tall, blonde and highly spirited, and her arrival distracted the Hasid. "Excuse me, Rabbi Winkler, I'll be right with you. Let me just help out this lady."

I remained in place and watched the Chabadnik approach the woman and ask her how he could help her. She explained to him that one of her daughters was falling under the influence of some evangelical Christian friends who were confusing her with proofs from the Jewish Bible that Jesus was the son of God and the true

Messiah, and she felt helpless as a mother because she was not learned enough in the Hebrew scriptures to rebuff the proofs and answer her daughter's many questions about Judaism. It reminded me of the so many parents and children in that situation that I had assisted over the years as a rabbi in New York. I recalled the 53-page single-spaced letter I had written to that young woman four months ago, and how this masterpiece manuscript had been rotting away in the trunk of my car for months because I didn't know what to do with it. It had been returned because the addressee had moved and had left no forwarding address.

The Hasid went to work showing the woman several titles that dealt with the subject of "How to answer missionaries" but they cost too much and the woman kept reciting over each book: "Oh, I don't know, that's too expensive."

"Pardon me," I blurted, walking over to where the woman was whining about prices. "But I happen to have this 53-page single-spaced letter I once wrote to a member of the Jews-for-Jesus movement. Maybe it would help your daughter, or help you to answer your daughter's questions. And you can have it for nothing."

The woman turned toward me, smiling with excitement while the Chabadnik proudly introduced me as "the famous author, Rabbi Gershon Winkler," to which the woman responded: "Wow, and from an author, yet. This is too good to be true. This is a real miracle from God. I've been praying so hard for one. This is too good to be true!"

She suggested I bring the manuscript to the office of this synagogue where she worked part-time so that she might copy it on the machine, refusing adamantly to take my only copy. I followed her to the synagogue, manuscript in hand, wishing she would have just taken the damn thing off my hands and left me alone so I could negotiate the Chabadnik for my sandwich. But she insisted, and I was too weak from hunger to argue. As she ran the pages through the copy machine I eyed her lustfully, fantasizing what it would be like to have her medium rare with a little ketchup on the side and a glass of Manischewitz. I was about to grab a letter opener and recite the prayer for ritual slaughter when she swerved around to face me with joy and excitement: "I can't believe it! This is really a miracle! God has really answered my prayer! I want to do something in return, if I could, like is it okay to invite you for dinner or something maybe tomorrow, or Thursday? I mean, you're probably very busy, being a rabbi and an author and all, but I feel like I want to somehow repay you."

"Miracles are free," I muttered weakly, my eyes locked on a jar of coffee sitting on an adjacent desk.

"Still. I would be really honored if you would come for dinner some night. Where are you staying?"

"Oh, uh … at the Beverly Hilton."

"The Beverly Hilton?! Wow. That's a real ritzy place, huh? What room are you in so I could call you to invite you to dinner, like maybe on Wednesday or Thursday?"

There was a pause for what seemed to be a long period of time. Schmuck! I thought to myself. Which is better? Surrendering to the very community from which you travelled so far to get way, and— worse yet—begging from a Chabadnik who knew all about you? Or confessing to a "Course in Miracles" devotee who only knew you were an author but didn't know much else about you?

"Actually," I broke down, "I was just kidding. I'm not staying at the Beverly Hilton. See that little red car down the block a bit? On the left? Well, uh …"

Her face turned deeply concerned. "You're not stranded, are you?"

I was silent. Could I tell her? This stranger? This angel who just rescued me from shame?

I *could* tell her, I felt. I *could* let go and tell this woman and not have to be embarrassed or save face or explain anything. Did this mean that my newly chosen life direction had been affirmed? After all, I was being given a way out of what I presumed was a forced return to the lifestyle I had abandoned. I thought I heard a Heavenly Voice proclaim: "I'm okay, you're okay." I told the lady, Yes I was stranded. She took me home, fed me fish and rice, gave me a room, and told me I could stay as long as I wanted, no strings attached. Her name was Sarah.

God exists. And there are angels. And neither God nor angels live in Heaven. Rather, they wander the earth looking for *schlemiels*.

Chapter Nine

Skeleton Woman

My belly was full. I had a place to sleep. But I was still horny.

In the morning I found Sarah on the phone with Dee, a woman who had fallen on bad times and was now destitute. Down and out. She was once a successful fashion designer, Sarah explained to me later, but now she was hungry. My initial instinct was to run over to West Hollywood and feed this poor woman. My secondary instinct was to run over to West Hollywood and make love to her. As I hurried to Dee's apartment on foot, I became aware of how I had been reduced to a peculiar species of animal that thrived on nothing other than food and sex, yearned for nothing other than food and sex, thought of nothing other than food and sex. I had in essence become the very kind of boorish person I used to abhor in my Orthodox days and about which I had always read discrediting statements in my studies of the sacred texts.

I passed the Chabad storefront along the way and had an evil idea.

"Ah! Rabbi Winkler!" declared my Hasidic fan, "I'm so glad you came back, I didn't get a chance to speak with you—you ran off so fast with that lady. You know, I wanted to ask you something: when you wrote *The Golem of Prague*, did you actually go to Prague to do your research?"

"Listen," I responded, "I'm in a kind of a hurry right now. See, there's this woman I just found out about who hasn't eaten in several days. You know, she's broke. So maybe you have some kind of fund to dip into so I could buy her some food? I'm in town for a short time and don't have any extra cash on me."

"What's the question?" said he, dipping into the register and withdrawing a twenty. It was the most money I'd seen in over a week. I had gotten a handout after all, I realized, but without losing face. What a God, what a God, I thought. And I could have sworn I heard a Heavenly Whisper echo back: "What a *schmuck*, what a *schmuck*."

I grabbed the twenty and bee-lined for the deli across the street where I bought Dee a whopping pastrami sandwich with the works, and a Dr. Brown's soda. Pocketing the change and feeling like a man of means once more, I walked briskly across the border into West Hollywood and headed for Dee's place. When I got there, an anorexic looking black woman sat on the stoop smoking a dwindling butt. She appeared extremely stoned but lucid. It was Dee. I told her Sarah had sent me to bring her this sandwich.

Dee staggered to her feet and hugged me with every bone in her emaciated body, then invited me up to her apartment. I accepted the invitation and followed her up the stairs inhaling the aroma of marijuana that spiraled downward from all the upper floors.

Once inside her web, I expected her to snarf up the sandwich and gasp for air and sigh with relief from finally having some food in her nearly visible gullet. Instead, she took a smidgen of a nibble the size of a chicken's peck and launched into a three-hour monologue about her life, harping primarily on her failed marriage and once-successful career. Having exhausted those topics she went into a tirade on how she was a born-again Christian but also "kind of Jewish," and then she proceeded to show me her fashion designs and offered me some brandy. I was too overwhelmed by her mind-spinning nonstop yakking to notice that we had somehow made it to her bed and that she had even at some point begun to wrap her bony arms around me and had started fondling parts of me I had come to assume were stone dead.

I was shocked back to reality when she suddenly ceased talking and shut her eyes. Her clothes were off and I found myself grovelling hungrily over her skin-draped skeleton, trying to find something to grab, something to hold on to, to touch and to feel. My search was in vain, although Dee was in bliss from being touched. As she swooned and moaned, I realized she had been starving alright, but not for pastrami, so I continued making love to this fragile cluster of skin and bones. As soon as she came she fell asleep and left me wondering what happened to the quality of my earnings in the World to Come now that I came.

Omigosh! What had I done? I began to feel guilty having had sex with a starving woman. Listen, some people enjoy a smoke or a snack after sex. And others, like me, enjoy an attack of guilt or anxiety. But I was really feeling bad, like what if she did it as payment for the sandwich I had bought her with Chabad money? Oh my God! This couldn't have happened! I immediately employed my skills of talmudic questioning and proofing: okay, lessee—she said she was a born-again Christian, but that had to be a lie because if it was true, she would never have had sex with me because we weren't married. So if that was a lie, then it is possible that the sex was a lie, too, and that it never really happened.

I got back into my clothes and sat on the bed caressing Dee's hair and forehead while thinking of all the stories in the Talmud of rabbis who succumbed to temptation and the kind of penance they did afterward. I decided my penance would be no sex whatsoever for at least an hour, including masturbation. I rose from the bed, shaken and feeling yucky. I hadn't asked for it, I hadn't even made a pass at her. Nonetheless, the ancient rabbis had been right about this one, too, that what I lusted for in my mind and heart was bound to become manifested in real life as well.

> In the way a person wishes to go,
>
> they are led
>
> **~ Babylonian Talmud, *Makot* 10b**

I never went back.

That night, lying in Sarah's meditation room, I realized that I needed to do some heavy re-evaluating of my life, of my theology, of who I was and where I wanted to go, not where I *was* going. I was starting to feel like a rolling stone, tumbling on and on and on down a hillside toward some brush. I mentioned this to some guy I met strumming his guitar on the sands of Venice Beach, whose name I think was Bob Dill ... something, I don't remember. Anyway, I felt like I needed to find a private space where I could find out what it was I *wanted,* not lusted. And once I found such a space, it would be great to invite a woman there to ...

There I go again. I just had sex, and my libido was still hungry.

> There is a small
> organ in the man.
> The more he feeds it,
> the hungrier it gets.
>
> **Babylonian Talmud, *Sukkah* 52b**

Chapter Ten

Milagro

> Miracles happen only when you're not expecting
> one, when you let go of ever having one happen to
> you. The Red Sea split because Moses threw up his
> arms in defeat, as is written: "And Moses stretched
> out his hands over the sea" (Exodus 14:27).
>
> **'ִ⊱ Talmud of the Schmelves [Jewish elves],**
> **tractate of *Baba Meises* 44e**

About a moon later I found the space I was looking for. A rustic old cabin deep in the Angeles National Forest overlooking a rushing creek. I had also found a freelance writing job with an L.A. Jewish tabloid, and with what they were paying me I was back on my feet enough to rent the cabin and start sending some money to the family in New York. The cabin had a light bulb but no plumbing, and an old pot belly stove was its sole source of heat whenever I fed it wood and newspapers. I was no country boy back then and so when I ran out of wood one chilly night I hacked to pieces some of the furniture lying around. I became notorious for burning furniture for firewood, and friends would watch me carefully when I would come into town to visit and drool over their furniture and wood sculptures.

In the beginning, living in the woods was to be a temporary venture while I figured things out. In the end, living in the woods became a lifestyle that I enjoy deeply to this day.

Slowly, I transformed from a city boy to a woodsman, chopping my own furni ... uh ... wood, hauling water up from the creek, bathing in the creek with biodegradable soap, hiking a half mile to my car, and showering during the summer months beneath a nearby waterfall much to the chagrin of passing tourists and scout troops. And like a real country boy I even had my regular run-ins with the forest ranger who kept pestering me to sweep up the dry leaves around the cabin to prevent a forest fire from happening. I compromised by purchasing a battery-operated smoke alarm.

The fine was about a hundred bucks.

Living in this cabin did not in any way help me arrive at any theological clarity, and I still had no idea whether what I was doing was right or wrong. What I did know and discover up there in the San Gabriel wilderness was that I didn't want to live in the city anymore. Never ever. I loved the feel of living in the wilds. It was peaceful, quiet, still, fragrant, and tranquil. I loved it so much that it no longer mattered whether slip-sliding away from orthodoxy was right or wrong. What mattered instead was my newfound truth: boonies.

"Hi, it's me. Gershon."

"Hello. Is everything okay?"

"Everything is perfect."

"Does this mean you're coming home?"

"No. It means I love living in the woods."

"Hmmm. Did you achieve any clarity about your direction?"

"My direction?"

"You know, the direction you were going, away from *frumkeit* (orthodoxy)."

"Oh that. Uh … actually, no. I've been too preoccupied with enjoying life in the woods."

"Gershon, you went away to think things through, to get some space away from everything and to contemplate what it is you are doing."

"True."

"So have you discovered anything? Reached any conclusions?"

"Yes. That I love living in the woods."

"I am prepared to pack us all up and join you in the woods, Gershon, but you have to promise me that in return you will come back to the Torah way."

"This *is* the Torah way. These woods. Every tree is a verse in the Torah, complete with rabbinic commentaries and midrashic interpretations."

"That's not what I meant. Will you stay Orthodox if we join you in the woods?"

"I honestly don't feel that I would. I'm sorry, but I really don't feel I want to go that way. I have a great affection for it, but I've outgrown that way of life. I'm somewhere else now and it feels right for me."

"I'm going to have to consult with the rabbis. You know, about what to do. I can't live with you like this, if you're going off the path."

"I understand."

"Thank you for the money you sent."

"No need to thank me. You guys are still my family, you know.

"When are you coming home?"

"I bought a plane ticket today. I'm coming to visit next Tuesday. Maybe stay a week."

"Good. The children will be very happy to see you."

"I will be very happy to see them, too, and to see you."

"You sound so different. Your voice. You must have been through a lot on this journey."

"I guess."

"We miss you."

"I miss you, too. All of you."

"Tuesday, then."

"Tuesday it is."

"Oh, one moment."

"Yes?"

"I just noticed on the calendar that Tuesday is *Tisha B'Av*."

Tisha B'Av is a day of grieving over the destruction of the Holy Temple in Jerusalem which fell in 69 c.e. Only one other event, the

ancient sages taught, is as sad to God as is *Tisha B'av*, and that is
the breaking up of a marriage (Babylonian Talmud, *Gitin* 90b).

Living in an Orthodox Jewish communtity all these years, I had
never needed to consult the calendar for upcoming festivals or fast
days. I just knew when everything was because the entire community knew. Call it collective consciousness, but it worked remark-
ably and comfortably well. No one ever forgot what holyday it was
or whether next Tuesday was going to be a major fast day. No one
but the bearded *yold* swinging from the trees of the Angeles National
Forest in Southern California.

I hung up and called a Jewish bookstore in Los Angeles to order
a Hebrew calendar.

Early the following *Wednesday*, I packed a modest suitcase for
my first post-New York visit to New York. The car had been gassed,
the oil changed, brand new tires, transmission fluid and filter changed,
and plenty of time to get to the airport in Los Angeles without rushing. The day felt good. I was a little nervous about this trip, but the
day felt good. Smooth. No hassles. God was with me, holding my
hand as I commenced the half mile trek along the creek to the Forest Service campground where my car was parked. I threw my bag
into the back seat, got in, shut the door, inserted the key into the
ignition, turned it ...

Nothing.

I turned it again.

Nothing. Nil. Zero. Totally dead.

This wasn't really happening. It couldn't be happening. I was
miles from a mechanic. Miles from my own personal public phone
booth in Altadena. Miles from a jumper cable. Miles from a prayer.
Pissed, I jumped out and started yelling at God.

"You've got a whole goddam universe to run and you have to
pick on *me* today? Don't you realize how important this trip is? I
mean, is there a dearth of wicked people in the world that you have
to specifically pick on me? And couldn't it wait till I got a little closer
to a gas station, or better yet, till I got back from my trip? What kind

of crap is this? What—you you you think this is funny? You think this is some kind of creative cosmic joke? Who the ..."

Just then I heard a rumbling in the distance.

"Haha. Just ... uh ... just kidding, O Mighty One, O Majestic Sovereign of the Universe. Many, *many* universes at that!"

The rumbling grew louder and louder.

"Yes ... uh ... O you who art above all that is, beyond all exaltation and praise, as is written ..."

The rumbling was now at an all time roar sending lizards and chipmunks scurrying for cover, and robins and finches to flight.

"Um ... uh ... you who art the highest of the high, exalted above all, while I, a mere worm, a mere amoebic glob, stand here in awe before your terrible ..."

It was a tow truck.

Honest to God. It was a tow truck, kicking up a storm of dust as it swerved up Chaney Trail to the campground, circled around the parking area, and screeched to a dusty halt several yards from my comatose car.

I stood there in shock and watched in astonishment as the burly mustached driver rolled down his window and greeted me, the cool breeze of his air-conditioned cab blowing across my bald, *yarmulka*-less head.

"Got a '65 Pinto up here?" he yelled.

"Uh uh," I replied, almost in a whisper, still in a trance-like state from the miracle that was happening before my very eyes, and right in the middle of my tirade against God. The Creator could at least have let me finish venting. I couldn't decide which was worse, the disabling of my car or the interruption of my cursing with a miracle, which made me look rather silly.

"Are you sure?" the mechanic shouted above the rumbling engine of his mud-caked truck.

"Yup. No one up here but me."

"That's strange. I got a call to come up here. Said there was a '65 Pinto up here that needed a boost or something."

"No Pinto up here. Just me and this old '77 Plymouth."

"Well, alright, then. Guess they got the location wrong."

He shouted a thank you at me, revved up his engine while rolling up his window, and started to take off when I realized that my miracle was going to pass right by me unless I took some immediate action. I waved my arms at him to flag him back. He threw the old truck into reverse and returned, rolling down his window as he approached.

"What's up, buddy?"

"Well, I was wondering if you could … you know, since you're here already anyway … if you could give me a boost. My car won't start."

"Shit, buddy, why didn't you say so? Sure thing. Beats my comin' allaway up here for nothin'."

He got my car started in less than no time, declined my offer of five bucks (a lot of money in the early eighties), and took off.

'65 Pinto my ass. Someone told me later there was no such thing as a '65 Pinto. An angel, then? No doubt, because only an angel would think there was such a thing as a '65 Pinto.

While we're busy cursing God, miracles are zooming by us in third gear. While we're busy asking, God is busy answering.

> And it shall come to pass
> that before they have even begun to call,
> I will already have answered;
> before they have even begun speaking,
> I will already have heard.

⁖ Isaiah 65:24

So I flew to New York, rented a car from Ugly Duckling Car Rentals, Inc., and drove home to my wife and kids. Seeing the girls melted me into a sticky puddle of gook. I wanted so badly to take them back to the woods with me but I knew that it would be best for them to stay with their mother and to continue to flourish uninterruptedly in the Orthodox world, the only reality grid they knew. Seeing Bryna threw me abruptly back into the reality I thought I had left behind, with an impact so powerful that I almost dropped to my knees before her to confess all my sins and to take a vow of eternal allegiance to her and Orthodox Judaism. Thank God vows are virtually proscribed altogether in traditional Jewish law, and that my knees were still painfully swollen from a fall I had taken a week earlier while making my way up the creek at night without a flashlight. (I'd been told I wouldn't need a flashlight during the full moon. What they didn't tell me was this did not apply when the skies were completely overcast.)

It would indeed have been the right thing to do, too, to confess the wrongness of my straying and to surrender myself to the warmth and sanctity that I experienced upon seeing the family again. I know in my gut that had I chosen to restore myself to orthodoxy in that moment, the Messiah would have come instantly. No questions asked. No holds barred. If nothing else it would have been an opportunity to show Christians how wrong they had been all these centuries. Damn. And I gave all that up. I gave it up because I was still in the middle of planting a fresh and fragile sapling of life unfolding.

> If you are holding a seedling in your hand and
> they tell you that the Messiah has arrived,
> first finish planting,
> then go and greet the Messiah.
>
> **1st-century Rabbi Yochanan ben Zakai in**
> **Babylonian Talmud, 2 *Avot d'Rebbe Natan* 31:2**

So there I stood, in the presence of the most beautiful family cluster on earth, my heart glomped to theirs, while fantasizing about how it would have been if only I'd have in that moment surrendered to them and brought the Messiah. How he would have set things straight for all of Christianity:

———————————

"If I am *the* redeemer, as you say, then what am I after the redemp-
tion is over? A has-been hero like John Glenn? Retired to do book sign-
ings and lecture tours? No, my sisters and brothers, wrong, wrong,
wrongo. Number one: I am not Jesus of Nazareth. I am Harry Hochberg
of Paramus. Number two: I have not come to do any kind of redeem-
ing, for the need to be redeemed is something you guys made up, not
God. Rather I have come to knock down the price of cable, to beat your
weapons into plowshares and pruning hooks so that when you go to
war with each other, it'll *really* hurt. I mean, those things are painful,
them plowshares and pruning hooks. Especially since you won't learn
about war anymore, which means you won't know how to use those
tools properly, which makes them all the more dangerous. I have also
come to do away with health insurance premiums, except for those who
still owe on theirs, and also I come to ..."

———————————

"Abba."

———————————

"... to ... to resurrect the dead, so you better relocate your asses
before some of your deceased creditors come stomping along like in
that movie 'Night of the Living Dead.' And also I have come to ..."

———————————

"Abba."
It was the voice of my oldest daughter, Miriam.
"Yes, precious."
"Are you going to stay?"

> Behold I send to you Elijah the Prophet before
> the great and awesome day of
> Infinite One shall come to pass.
> And he shall restore the hearts of
> the parents to the children and
> the hearts of the children to their parents,
> lest I come and delete the whole shebang.

❧ Book of Malachi 3:24

"I love you so deeply. I want to be with you always."

"So are you staying?"

"You are more important to me than anything in the world."

"So are you staying?"

"You think I can ever forget all those diapers I changed when you were an infant?"

"So, Abba, are you staying?"

"Or the countless nights when you were colic-y, how I carried you on my shoulders for hours, singing to you until either one of us fell asleep?"

"Does that mean you're staying?"

"No. It only means that I'm not leaving you."

"Then you *are* staying."

"Not staying, just not leaving either. I will never leave you. But I cannot live where it is best for you to live. I am unhappy here. I am happy where I am."

"In California?"

"No. It isn't only about geography. It is about where in my life direction that I now find myself. If I were to force myself to be where I once was, I would be dying inside and no good to you as a father. No good to anyone. No good to your mother as a husband."

"But if you don't live with us, what good will you be as a husband then?"

"Better no husband than a zombie one, my daughter. I am sorry this is happening. Maybe one day you will understand my decision. Maybe you won't. But in any event, I can't stay."

"You *can't*, or you don't want to?"

Once, after Rabbi Yisroel Baalshem Tov (18th century) had finished teaching, a nobleman approached him and chastised him for his ridiculous teachings. "You are an embarrassment to me. The other dukes in the province ridicule me on account of your preposterous teachings. I order you to desist!" Said Rabbi Yisroel: "Which

teachings? Give me an example." Said the duke: "Like
the one I heard today, that everything you see or hear is
a message from God. Why that's ridiculous! I can't
accept such a notion!" Said Rabbi Yisroel: "You can't?
Or, you don't want to?" "I can't!" "Again, Your
Excellency, you can't, or you don't want to?" The duke
left in disgust, murmuring some anti-Jewish epithets
beneath his breath as he mounted his steed and took
off. Half way home, he came upon a peasant who was
struggling to right his overturned wagon. "Your
Excellency," pleaded the peasant, "seeing that there is
none else to help me, would you please assist me in
pushing my wagon back onto its wheels?" The duke
became furious at the suggestion, and shouted:
"Of course not! I can't do any such thing!" To which the
peasant replied: "You can't? Or, you don't want to?"

❦ Heard from Rabbi Shlomo Carlebach

The uncomfortable piece to my New York visits was the judg-
mental eyes of neighbors gazing at me as I transferred from the rental
car to the house. I was one of those recalcitrant husbands, a man
who had abandoned his wife and children in pursuit of selfish, personal desires. I was a man who had put his own dreams and whims
before the emotional and relationship needs of his family, a man
who had strayed from the only true path to follow after his own
heart and its foibles. I was a man who was well-versed in all of the
Talmudic and medieval warnings about the Evil Inclination; a master who had won every battle against temptation during three gruelling years in the military—and now had fallen head first into the
very grasp of that very impulse.

I had become a pariah—but mostly in my own mind, in my own
projection and assumption. In truth, however, the gazes were more
looks of astonishment and puzzlement than of judgments. How could

someone like myself, steeped and marinated in orthodoxy, a hero in the war against assimilation and unorthodoxy, suddenly leave the fold? The community was now more frightened than ever before of the Evil Inclination and his insurmountable power, and the more respectful of the warnings of the sages of yore. See? Even such a one as the venerable Rabbi Gershon Winkler is not safe from the clutches of the Evil One.

> One who is more spiritually evolved
> than his fellow, is also that much more
> vulnerable to the Evil Inclination.
>
> **Babylonian Talmud, _Sukah_ 52a**

Bryna realized that this marriage could not be saved, yet she chose to heed the counsel of the rabbis, who advised her against divorcing me since they felt that I was most probably just going through "a phase." So for two years she put her life on hold as my "phase" birthed yet more phases and didn't appear to be waning.

My mother could not fathom my transformation and thought I was nuts, mostly for wearing plaid shirts and jeans. My father, on the other hand, in his extraordinary way, took it in stride, accepting my unfolding in spite of how different I was becoming from his hopes for me. Often I wonder if he indeed ever so much as entertained _any_ hopes for me or for anyone else in his comfortable "live and let live" mindset.

For me, my father remained always the walking, living, breathing embodiment of everything Judaism had taught about the attributes of God: compassionate, joyful, caring, patient, tolerant, truthful, respectful, understanding, non-demanding, and negotiable.

> Says the Compassionate One:
> "Just do. And whatever it is
> you find to do, is pleasing to Me."
>
> **Babylonian Talmud, _B'chorot_ 17b**

Chapter Eleven

The Aquarian Conspiracy

We are sperm,

dancing in the tunnel,

as we squirm

and wiggle through the funnel,

toward the egg,

floating in suspension,

on our last leg

as we approach with apprehension;

'cuz we're not sure

we want someone else's totem,

which is what's in store

once we leave the scrotum.

ancient aboriginal schmelvic chant

The sperm dance was one of my many inventions of forms of entertainment to preserve in my daughters the lightness of being even in a bent family. Not broken, not fractured, just pretty bent out of shape. There was no animosity, no ill will between Bryna and myself. She didn't poison the children's minds against their *meschuggeneh* rabbi-turned-mountainman father. She didn't preach to them about the evils of my unorthodox ways. And thank God they are today happily married with good, solid, stable husbands, and a couple of kids each, and we enjoy a beautiful relationship even though our respective theologies are worlds apart; a relationship that has continued joyful, secure, and unbroken from that fateful summer in 1982 to the present.

But little did they know that the sperm dance was more than this silly dance we did whenever I flew in for one of my week-long visits. The sperm dance was a life dance that swept me, like sperm, away from my obsessive struggle with the Evil Inclination into the alluring albeit discriminating ovum of the Sirens that comprised a good portion of a funky Jewish congregation in Berkeley, California, called the Aquarian Minyan.

Having left the orthodoxic way of Jewishing, I had also put behind me any notion of continuing as a rabbi, as a teacher. I felt that I had fallen from grace as they say, unworthy of being called Rabbi, unworthy of ever again teaching so much as a word of Torah to another mortal. It felt sort of like an exchange, a trade-off, in return for which I was spared the actual enormity of the guilt that I was suppressing further and further every step of the way away from The Way.

But back in Los Angeles, Sarah the Angel refused to let go of me as a rabbi. After all, she knew my secret. She knew that I had written all these books, and that the Chabad guy on Fairfax referred to me as *Rabbi* Winkler since word hadn't reached him yet about my clipped wings. And so, during one of my visits with Sarah, she had some friends over and in the course of rambling conversations various theological questions got posed and the dormant rabbi in me got triggered like I was some kind of werewolf suddenly shifting from mortal to supernal, fangs beginning to grow out of my mouth, fur over my body, claws in the place of my nails, and deep talmudic scholarship in the place of my nonchalant and irreverent mountainmanliness. I found myself explaining Torah as I would back in Brooklyn, in my light way, with humor, with a quality of logic that was attractive to my audience, and they lapped it up thirstily, brimming for more.

Wow, I thought, I was still able to teach Torah even from where I was at *now*, even from having drooled after prostitutes up and down Hollywood Boulevard and running around the woods without covering my head. Wow. Had I indeed defeated—no, outsmarted—the Evil Inclination? Had he finally finally finally left me alone? Could I now return to rabbi'ing from this newly evolving plane of theology without having to struggle further with that crazy, pestering sonofabitch?

Then, as I was about to head back to the jungle, a woman came up to me and thanked me for the teachings, for the explanations and answers to all her questions. Would I like to participate in a retreat? It's called "The Joys of Jewishing." And it's held in the woods up in the Sierras. And it's put together every summer by "The Aquarian Minyan." It would be great if I could make it. I have a lot to offer.

Wow. A new niche had been carved for me by God so that I might continue as the great, venerable, holy master that I was; so that I didn't have to sell any more of my soul to the Evil Inclination in return for guilt-free transgressions of the Torah; so that I didn't have to fall any lower than I had until now. It sounded wonderful. I said Yes. In my mind I ripped to shreds the bill of sale handed to me several months earlier by the Evil One. I had bought back my soul. I was holy again, clean, and ready to resume the service of God Almighty.

And so, within a month, I found myself deep in the backwoods of the Sierras ritually immersing my sex-tainted body in the cleansing, purifying waters of a gentle river, surrounded by towering redwoods and about twenty stark naked women bellowing Hebrew liturgical chants. And in the distance, perched atop a stony overhang, the Evil Inclination sat laughing and laughing and laughing while taping together our shredded contract.

> Day by day does the Evil Inclination seek to overcome a person. If it cannot overcome him in ten years, it seeks then to overcome him in twenty years. Even if there is only one opportunity in *eighty* years, it seizes it!
>
> *Midrash Tanchuma, B'shalach* **28a**

But the Sirens of the Aquarian Minyan did more than conjure up lewd thoughts in my otherwise pure mind: they humbled my ego while raising my libido. Graciously they provided me with the hope, but only the hope, of the intimacy I so longed for. The price for following these Sirens into the sea of uncertainty and of alluring promises was the cost of challenging my mindset which was still thoroughly locked into the very paradigm I thought I had transcended by now. They challenged my patriarchic views of the feminine, my masculine expectations of womanhood, and the gynophobic quality of my teachings. They challenged my stuckness, my hesitation around marinating my traditional wisdom with the innovative insights waiting to be harvested from my new place of being.

I thought I had found some women to just play with. Instead I returned from the Sierras with my heart and gut turned topsy-turvy from challenges to my existential authenticity posed by a coven of wisewomen. Rather than stay away from these arrow-sharp goddesses, however, I kept going back to them for more sparks, more heart-wrenching homework for my spiritual unfolding. More than sensual bliss, these wild ladies gave me the gift of discovering, however difficult, my own power and wisdom.

I had become a feminist. And I hated every minute of it. And so did the Evil Inclination who now had to contend not only with me but also with the Felines of Berkeley who were reprogramming my reality map around women, sexuality, and relationshiping. I mean, just when I had gotten freed up to engage in rampant unbridled sex across state lines, the Sexual Revolution was coming to an abrupt end.

It disappointed me to no end to learn that while I had been spending all those years immersed in Torah and prayer, the rest of the world had been immersed in no-holds-barred lovemaking. And now, just when I was ready to join the Sexual Revolution, its female veterans had abandoned us perpetually needy men to revolt against the Patriarchy!

No longer could I simply jump into bed with any willing remnants of the Flower Children era. Instead, much to the chagrin of my libido and the Evil Inclination, I was being trained toward a whole new respect for women and a whole new way of thinking about them.

"That was a really nice hike we had, Gershon. I really like you a lot."

"It *was* a good hike. And I feel really close to you."

"I feel that way about you, too.

"Wow."

"Ummm … would you like to stay over?"

"I'd *love* to."

"You could sleep in *my* bed, if you want."

"Wow. I want, I want!"

"Good. I'll sleep on the sofa."

And thus did it come to pass that the Evil Inclination and I wandered aimlessly amid the rubble of a fallen Patriarchy, sobbing hand in hand, and desperately seeking the counsel of Robert Bly and Iron John. The world was changing rapidly behind my back, without my input, and long before I could catch up with it.

Life back in the Yeshiva World had been so much simpler. Nothing changed on you, everything was predictable, and far more sensual than what the late eighties were becoming for the so-called enlightened "outside" world. Jewish tradition had for thousands of years understood and honored women's need for sexual space from even their husbands.

> A man should not hover around
> his woman like a rooster.
>
> **Maimonides: *Mishnah Torah,*
> *Hil'chot De'ot* 5:4**

To this day, women and men in the Orthodox Jewish tradition shift once a month from intimate partnering to platonic partnering, about two weeks on and about two weeks off, the off time beginning with the woman's menstrual time, or, in ancient Hebrew: *nidah,* which means Cycle of Solitude. The world was now done with its "two weeks on" and was entering its "period of solitude." Both women and men were turning inward and away from one another, leaving Johnny-come-lately *schmeggegs* like me out in the cold. Now, it was either engage someone in serious, long-term, committed relationship, or writhe in painful, eternal abstinence. Daughters of the Sexual Revolution were rapidly becoming walking time bombs, their biological clocks ticking away so loudly that men were fleeing in all directions like lemmings from brushfire.

I know. I am being dramatic. But this is how it felt for me, this major transition, that while I was becoming uninhibited the world around me was becoming frigid; that as I was dropping my inhibitions, the world around me was picking them up.

I was basically being re-introduced by the non-Orthodox world to everything I had been raised with in the *Orthodox* world, from perceiving women as other than sex objects, to not taking relationships with them for granted, to relating with women without fantasizing what it would be like sleeping with them. All this stuff was stuff I had studied in the millennia old religious teachings of Judaism. I had not rejected this mindset but had rather misplaced it in my zeal to break through the barriers that I felt were restricting my aliveness.

Ironically, as I was putting more and more miles between myself and orthodoxy, the so-called Jewish progressive and renewal movements were reverting that much closer to the very orthodoxy that I had left behind. The more I leaned toward the left, the more the rest of the world leaned toward the right. Just when I was starting to take my yarmulka off, Reform Jews were starting to put theirs on. By the time I'd arrived, everyone else had been long gone.

> Oh, every time I go south, the world goes north,
> And everytime I push back, they all push forth.
> Things always seem to come up, when I sit down,
> And ever'one's seems to be out, when I'm in town.

song: 1985

In the summer of 1985, I split.

Once again I was on the run. This time from *non*-Orthodox voices bent on thwarting my liberation, although my primary draw eastbound was my growing daughters who I was feeling were in need of more father time as they were maturing. Or perhaps it was I who was in need of more *children* time as *I* was maturing.

> More than does the calf wish to suckle,
>
> does the cow wish to nurse.
>
> **Babylonian Talmud, *P'sachim* 112a**

As I had three years ago left the east coast for the west, I was now leaving the west coast for the east. I needed some space from all this transitioning, from the omnipresence of the re-emerging Goddess. I needed some time to grieve the fall of the Patriarchy within, and to figure out once again where I was going and what I was becoming. The reconnection with Jewish community—the radical flavor of the Aquarian brand notwithstanding—had been premature. I needed more time. I needed to *not* be doing rabbi stuff. I needed to *not* rethink the way I taught because I really didn't want to teach anymore altogether! My well-intentioned romance with rabbi'ing for the Jewish Renewal folk up in Berkeley, I realized, had come more from an unhealthy desire to redeem myself for having left the orthodoxic version of it behind. It had been sort of like rabbi'ing on the rebound. And the little cabin in the Angeles National Forest had not been as far away from everything as I now felt it should have been. I needed further clarity, more remoteness.

Once again I broke some hearts, this time of some really nice women who wanted my children. But I wasn't ready for another marriage, certainly not ready for more parenting, and certainly not at all interested in any long-term or even short-term committed monogamy. I was just starting to feel my oats, to run amok in the fields with the Evil One, dancing my libido to crescendos I'd never known but had often fantasized about. To settle down with any one woman at this point would mean my demise. If the alternative was celibacy and loneliness—so be it.

> At twenty, a man is like a stallion, running about hither and thither. When he marries he becomes like a donkey, saddled with the burdens of supporting his wife and building a home. When he has children, he becomes as a dog, running desperately and shamelessly to and fro in search of sustenance, driven from place to place, taking from here and bringing to there, and from there to bring to here.
>
> *Midrash Tanchuma, P'kudei*

I returned to the east to be closer to my kids, but not too close to the world I'd originally left behind, especially since I'd become deeply addicted to rural living. So I settled in the backwoods of the southern branch of the North Fork River in the central region of eastern West Virginia near a tiny town called Romney—a gruelling 8-hour drive from the 2nd Avenue Deli. There, along a rushing creek, I rented an old one-bedroom trailer on a two-trailer trailer court run by a woman held hostage with well over one hundred-and-fifty channels bouncing off a satellite dish powerful enough to receive incoming signals from extraterrestrials.

> Satellite, satellite,
> I watch it all day and I watch it all night.
>
> *Country Western Song*

For a mere $125 a month, I now lived in this little red and yellow tin whose window faced a second trailer that was vacant. No one in their right mind would rent from this woman, so I qualified. I mean, this lady would change the locks on me whenever I was away for a spell visiting my children in New York, fearing that I'd perhaps abandoned it and given the key to someone else.

I moved out here 'cuz I love the state that's almost heaven,
love the feelin' of the freedom jus' to roam,
but ever' time I go honky-tonkyin' or to Seven-Eleven,
you sneak by and change my lock 'fore I get home.

One night I brought home this pretty woman I'd just met
and put my key into the lock but it don't go.
I started to explain but it was too late'n she got upset.
She said: "Take me home and don't you call on me no mo'."

O please don't change the lock on my door no more,
'cuz ever' time I go out I can't get in.
When I get back at night I'm pretty tired'n a lil' sore,
so please don't change the lock on my door no more.

🎵 Song: 1985

I had really done it this time, isolating myself from any degree of any kind of community with which I could in any shape or form relate. Way out here in true-blue redneck country there was not a single Jew in sight, or any trace of anyone remotely acquainted with one. And the job opportunities in the area numbered even less than the number of Jews. (Well, a few years later I did meet Hank Koppel, a Jewish accountant turned Angus farmer, who still does my taxes. Hi, Hank, the information you requested is in the mail.)

I had to think fast. How to earn an income while living along U.S. 50 in some remote region of West Virginia.

The answer came to me one day while I was shoveling shit in a sheep barn at the onset of lambing season. The answer was Jack Goldman, bless his soul, the publisher of Judaica Press, Inc. in Brooklyn. He had published my first several books. I could maybe squeeze an advance out of him toward yet another book. I could and I would, and I did on one of my visits to my kids.

The idea for this next book had been inspired back in Los Angeles by Miriam Huttler, wife of an L.A. rabbi. She had told me about the legendary Chanah Rochel Webermacher, an early nineteenth-century eastern European Chassidic woman rebbe, or spiritual leader. A controversial figure in Jewish lore and history, this woman had attracted a myriad of followers from across Poland and the Ukraine, upsetting the otherwise all-male rabbinate that comprised the Orthodox Jewish world back then. She was also known as a kabbalist, a faith healer, and a miracle worker. I decided to dig up the available crumbs of historical footnotes about this heroine and grind them into an historical novel. Jack loved the idea and sent me back to the hills with some cash and a cause.

West Virginia, it turned out, had been a good move, an intelligent choice on my part. No way in hell that anyone was going to drag me back into rabbi'ing from these very remote hollers. I was safe. Here I had finally discovered the tranquility of total anonymity, working on a sheep farm, writing a book, walking in the woods, and socializing with people whose only notion of the Jew was some ancient, long extinct Christ-killing demon memorialized in Sunday School folklore and passionate Easter church sermons. Surrounded by a culture completely alien to anything I knew and completely oblivious to my sojourn amidst its adherents, I typed out the novel of the lone woman rebbe who chose against all odds to live her life as *she* visioned it, not as others had planned it for her. From morning to evening I sat there in the rainstorm of autumn 1985 hammering away at my old manual typewriter while studying notes and research documents from Yivo Institute. This was the life.

Yes, my friends, I was finally free from my calling. No one could find me here. When the Jewish Renewal folks in Boulder, Colorado wrote asking me to come do a week of teaching, I simply ignored them. Nice try. They had heard about me from the Aquarian Minyanites back in Berkeley. Even here in what they called "Almost Heaven,"

God could not find me to compel me back to my rabbinic calling. But where Jonah had failed, I had succeeded. The ancient Hebrew prophet had attempted nobly to flee his calling, to run away from the mission that God had assigned to him, only to be thrown into raging waters, swallowed by a big fish, and then spat out on the shores of Nin'veh where he was supposed to have gone, to begin with. There may not have been any escape from his calling for Jonah the Prophet, but for Gershon the Winkler there was. Maybe Jonah hadn't tried hard enough. Tsk, tsk, tsk.

Within a few days of relentless rainfall, my trailer began to move ever so gently off its foundation of wooden blocks and into the neighboring creek that had by this time swollen to a full size river fit for whitewater rafting. I grabbed my manuscript, threw it into a half-filled suitcase, jumped out of the trailer into knee-deep water spilling out of the raging creek.

> And so they picked up Jonah and threw him into
> the sea, and the sea stopped raging.
>
> **ﯼ Book of Jonah 1:15**

Realizing that the water was rising rapidly, I climbed to the top of my car and waited. A helicopter hovered somewhere in the rain clouds above, and after an hour or so a motorboat arrived down U.S. 50 to pick me up. They had a tough time severing my landlady from her house across the road because she insisted on first chasing down my floating house to change the lock.

In Romney, I helped out at the fire station, attending to dozens of families who had lost their homes to this major major major flood. After three exhausting days and nights there, it began to dawn on me that I'd lost everything, and that I was homeless. All I had was a small suitcase with some underwear, some socks (I had never unpacked), my near-completed manuscript about the woman rebbe, and ninety bucks in cash.

They closed the bridge to Romney,
Moorefield's all but gone.
I live in the middle
'tween a hard place and a stone.
I walk fifteen miles for food and drink
'cuz my car got washed away.
Even lost m'sense of humor,
so there's nothin' left to save my day.
Oh, now the postman off'n gone fishin'
in what used to be the general store.
The banker, he off'n went canoin'
on what used to be his livingroom floor.
And the flood-insurance man up in Keyser—
they saw him paddlin' on a floatin' fridge;
but by the time the army found him,
he was clingin' to the Cacapon Bridge.

Was expecting a check from Petersburg,
but the town got washed away.
But what would I do with my money now,
when there ain't no one 'round to pay
and a billboard sign floatin' on the water
says "Ban will help me stay dry."
The storm's died down, the rain's become a drizzle,
I don't know if I should laugh or cry.

Tell me, O river, why'd you turn my life around?
Why'd you flow over and wash away my town?
You took ever'thing I worked for—there ain't nothin' left to sell.
You made Almost Heaven look like hell

✌§ Song: 1985

This was crazy. I'd just gotten here. I'd just been here a few months. I was just starting to acquire a southern accent, and then I get flooded out. I had no idea of what my next move ought to be, but the Evil Inclination had some interesting ideas, like maybe I could call this woman I knew who lived in Reston, Virginia. I met her in California and she'd invited me to stay with her if I were ever out her way. Good plan, provided, of course, I could get a ride to the nearest bus depot which was twenty two miles north in Cumberland, Maryland.

> And Infinite One prepared for Jonah
>
> a great fish to swallow Jonah.
>
> **◀ Book of Jonah 2:1**

On that third night I walked up and down Main Street looking for a way to get to Cumberland. Then:

"Got a cigarette?"

I turned to face the Adam's apple of a tall young guy with a cigarette perched behind his ear.

"Seems to me like you already have one," I said.

"Oh. Stupid of me. Where you headed with that suitcase?"

"Well, I'm trying to get to Cumberland. Have you got a car? I'll give you twenty bucks to drive me there."

"Well. My friend's got a car. Why don't you wait here a bit and I'll go see if he wants to do it."

In twenty minutes an old Plymouth showed up. The tall guy sat in the back seat and waved me into the front seat. The driver took off toward Cumberland. It was quiet. Too quiet. Suddenly the car took a sharp turn off the road and up a dirt road into the woods. I felt a belt wrap around my throat from behind, and a blunt instrument shoving at my spine through the back of my seat. As the belt tightened around my throat, the tall guy threatened my life if I tried to resist. He then ordered me out of the car, shouted to the driver to get the gun, and then proceeded to strip me of my jacket, my driver's license, and my ninety bucks. The two then took off, leaving me in the dark forest shivering from cold and trembling from fright. Chilled, wet, scared, and penniless, I was nonetheless thankful to be alive and unharmed. But they got my suitcase with my manuscript.

> Then did Jonah pray from inside the belly of the fish, and he said: "I cried out to you from the belly of the netherworld, and you heard my voice. For it is you who threw me into the abyss, into the heart of the waters; and the flood was round about me. All your waves and billows passed over me. And I declared: 'I am thrown out from before your eyes!' ... The waters surrounded me, even to the soul; the deep was all around me; the weeds were wrapped around my head. I went down to the very lowest parts of the mountains ... But you brought my life back up from the pit ..."
>
> **ᴥ Book of Jonah 2:2-7**

In the distance, not too far from the crime scene, I spotted the lights of a farm house. I made my way through the brambles and trees, down and up a flooded ravine, and finally to the road. I crossed the road to the farm house and knocked on the front door. When the farmer came to the door I asked him to call the police. He hesitated, himself in shock at the sight of a ghost in shirt sleeves shaking in the cold night air, and then disappeared back into the house. Within five minutes a State Police car appeared.

> And Infinite One spoke to the fish and it spat out Jonah onto the dry land.
>
> **ᴥ Book of Jonah 2:11**

The State Police took me in, got the details, kept me warm, and less than an hour later returned with both culprits in cuffs. Turned out they were troublemakers from Baltimore who had come to the flooded hills in search of prey. I pressed charges of armed robbery the next day at a Magistrate's hearing, and the bail was set at $250,000. They had to keep my driver's license and money as state's evidence, but they did award me my attacker's winter jacket and about a hundred other dollars in cash that they found on his person. A month later the state further awarded me three hundred dollars from its victim's compensation fund. My belongings, however, had been burned in the woods. That meant the manuscript was gone, too, and that I'd have to start Chanah Rochel all over again.

Okay, so I got the message. Okay, okay, so I ended up going to Boulder to teach after all. Okay, okay, okay, so I was no more successful in escaping my calling than was Jonah. Big deal. Picky, picky, picky.

And Infinite called to Jonah a second time, saying:

"Arise and go to Nin'veh ..."

◄§ Book of Jonah 3:1

Chapter Twelve

Cowboys and Hittites

I'd always dreamed of living in the wild west, Boulder wasn't quite that, but I stayed in town for a few months because I had lost everything, needed time to recuperate from the West Virginia episodes, and the fledgling Jewish renewal community in Boulder was skillfully putting me back together again. I was back to teaching and rabbi'ing and earning some incoming income.

Boulder was secure. It was a haven, a respite from all my wanderings. It felt good.

Look. Who am I kidding. This book is about my travels with the Evil Inclination. You see, what kept me in Boulder was *more* than the security of a livelihood, and *more* than the ego-boosting I got from a community of women and men who loved me and who shared a collective vision of my one day evolving into their full-time spiritual leader.

What kept me in Boulder was the discovery that the Sexual Revolution hadn't ended there yet, was still going on, was still vibrant. And that I was wanted for reasons beyond the rabbinate. So I succumbed. What, after all, is a man to do? At first it was flattering, floundering with several paramours simultaneously, but soon it became emotionally overwhelming, for a guy who hadn't a clue about how to relate to *one* woman, let alone four.

I've got a little problem 'cuz I know a lot of women, see,
in almost every city and town,
and the traffic's been gettin' kinda heavy just lately,

so I'm thinkin' of goin' underground.

For example, I got two women friends in two different cities

and both of them are expectin' me tonight,

and I promised a third that I would be right over,

so you can see how things are really gettin' tight.

Now I don't exactly know how all this happened,

got no time to figure it out.

I guess it all started when I got a little curious

and wanted to know what women was all about.

So I met one gal and then I met another

and the more I met the gladder I was,

until it reached a point, you see, when each of them would tell me:

"Why honey, I'm glad it's just us."

Oh I would try to explain to each and every one

that she wasn't the only one that I had.

Some didn't mind it, some were disappointed,

and the others, well, they got a little mad.

It got so bad that I'd take one of them to breakfast

and I'd meet the one I'm gonna take to brunch,

and then I'm sure as likely to meet my date for dinner

while I'm settin' with another havin' lunch.

So I'm in a really big bind and I'm a losin' my mind

and I've gotta think of some kind of solution,

'cuz I love 'em all and I sure don't wanna lose 'em

and the last thing I need's a revolution.

So I decided to see a psychoanalyst of sorts

to sorta sort this whole mess through,

but I don't gotta tell you, when I showed for my appointment,

— well, the doctor, she was one of them, too!

Cowboys and Hittites

I guess my situation has just got to be accepted
or I'm bound to live a life of misery,
but in spite of all the problems there's one consolation
that my love life will go down in history.
And I know that when I'm dead there'll be talk behind my back
about the epitaph my girls'll write for me:
"We shared this man, made him give us all he had
and left him nothin' but a lone eternity."

ﷺ Song: 1986

I had had it.

I was living a lie again. Here I was rabbi'ing and teaching when
I was still on vacation from walking the talk, and the lie was being
buffered by the bliss of being wanted dead or alive by women yet
untouched by the great storms of AIDS, abstinence, and monogamy
that had struck the west coast and was gradually looming over the
Rockies. The Evil Inclination had skillfully eased me into city living
with the lure of the aggressive and uninhibited Sirens of Boulder,
drowning my dreams and newfound rural self in the raging flood-
waters of West Virginia.

___

"Ay, Gershen, Gershen, Gershen."

___

It was the haunting voice of my teacher again, the voice of the
old man with the long unkempt white beard, long dead yet very
much alive in my conscience throughout my travels with the Evil
Inclination. Outside, it was hailing. The clock by my nightstand
claimed it was three in the morning. Lying beside me on the floor
mattress was the Goddess in Everywoman, peacefully asleep and
looking more sensual than when awake.

___

"Rebbe? Is that you?"
"It's not her, yes? So it must be me, no?"

"In Boulder? What are you doing in Boulder?"

"Listen, when one is as dead as I am, it matters little whether one is in Boulder or in Jerusalem. From here it all looks the same."

"You mean, Jerusalem is *not* the holiest city in the world?"

"Holy shmoly. From up here every place is holy."

"But why here? Why are you in Boulder?"

"Listen, that's *my* question for you."

"Why am *I* in Boulder?"

"Yes, why are *you* in Boulder?"

"You will be proud of why I am in Boulder. You can finally be proud of me, Rebbe. I am in Boulder because the Jews here asked me to be their rabbi, their teacher. I teach them Torah, bring them closer to God, and inspire them with the wisdom of our ancient sages."

"Listen, those ancient sages, they want to know who's that in bed with you."

"Where? Her? Me? She? Uh ... "

"Stop braying like a donkey. Does she menstruate?"

"Of course she menstruates."

"Has she immersed herself in living waters since her last period?"

"Well, I, she ... "

"Do you just sleep with anyone anytime?"

"You uh ... I ... she ... well ... uh ... "

"Is nothing sacred to you anymore?"

"Oh? To me? I ... uh ... well, I mean ... "

"Has the Evil One finally caught you?"

"Him? He ... uh ... no, no ... you, um ... "

"Is this the ordination I conferred upon you? To follow your *pupick*? To use your knowledge and rabbinic title as a means of becoming some kind of guru? As a tool for self-preservation and satisfaction? To pilfer from the till?"

"Oh nononono, you have me figured all wrong, Rebbe, I ... "

"Have I really? If you were not so charismatic in their eyes, would you be living here all these weeks? Would that woman have been badgering you these past three weeks to sleep with her?"

"I ... I ... I ... she ... I ... um ... no. I would probably be living up in those snowcapped alps, fixing fences and herding flocks. And this woman would have probably turned down so much as a lunch date with me."

There was a pause for what seemed to be a long period of time.

"Are you disappointed with me, Rebbe?"

"Over which piece?"

"My sleeping with a woman who hasn't performed ritual immersion since her last period?"

"Period, shmeriod. Up here it's all the same. Birth blood, menstrual blood, all the same. All is holy, all is pure. Every state of being, every cycle of life, is sacred. Each has its own sanctity, but all is sacred. But I am disappointed about something else."

"Yes, Rebbe?"

"Your dishonesty."

"My dishonesty? I don't understand."

"You cheated this woman and all the others. Because they are drawn to someone you are *pretending* to be, not to whom you truly are."

The Rebbe was right. Who was I kidding? I was playing dangerously with an entire community of sincere seekers who were harboring high hopes and long-range dreams around someone I had no intentions of becoming. I had the knowledge, the background, the experientials. I could easily feign the rabbinic leadership they were looking for toward the evolution of their fledgling alternative community. And I was attracting women who wanted to be with me, not women with whom I, too, wanted to be. And those with whom I *did* want to be, wisely wanted no part of me. I was a walking facade, a transient snake-oil salesman with nothing to offer but promises. I didn't even carry any order forms.

So one day, I announced to the Boulderites that I really needed to go back to the mountains. And to their utter disappointment, I did. At first, they assumed that I would at the very least come to town weekly to spend the Sabbaths with them, lead services, impart wisdom. But once up in them thar' hills, my passion for country living emerged once more. The idea of leaving the wilderness for the city made no more sense than a fish leaving the water for the shore.

I landed a job as a ranch hand on the Double-K Ranch (the Triple-K wouldn't have me) not far from the tiny dirt-road town of Rollinsville whose sole sign of aliveness was the notorious cowboy hang-out called The Stage Stop Inn. There, after a good day's work I would join the other ruffians for a long evening of drinks, cussing, tall tales, drinks, and cussing. Oh yes: and a whole lot of peeing. Then, whoever was least drunk would pile the others into the back of an old pickup and drive home.

Not being into the bunk house kind of way of lodging, I rented a small primitive cabin beside an old road while I went around letting people know I was looking for an even more secluded living situation.

When I wasn't at The Stage Stop, I would be in my cabin trying to resurrect the lost novel about the lost episodes of Chanah Rochel of Ludomir, that nineteenth century Chassidic woman rebbe. *Rebbe*, as opposed to *Rabbi*, is more of a kind of personal, downhome flavor of Rabbi. You know, the kind of rabbi the folks down in Boulder were hoping I would become. But alas, I was out of range. Once in a while I would come down, teach a little, gather up the cash from the voluntary contributions basket, and split. The Evil One had thrusted me into a mountainman mentality where nothing much mattered but survival and beer buddies. Heck, soon I was writing songs and singing them at the nearby Sundance Saloon in return for a free six-pack which I usually gave away to those for whom beer was a primary sustenance. The Stage Stop had no venue for singing rabbis, lacking both a stage and anyone sober enough to listen.

Not living in Boulder anymore was slowly becoming for me akin to asceticism. The chances of finding a girlfriend in the remote wilds of the then still underpopulated eastern Rockies was as good as finding lemonade at the Stage Stop. Actually, when I think back, I stood more of a chance finding lemonade there than a vacant urinal.

So life was rugged, rowdy, and exhilirating, but meaningless and asexual. Heck, even those fortunate enough to be coupled up were probably too inebriated most of the time to have sex anyway. Basically, then, I was living in a community of ascetics. This was very un-Jewish.

> Said Rabbi El'azar Ha'Kapar (2nd century): "Why did the avowed ascetic have to bring a sin offering at the conclusion of his vow of abstention? Because he painfully abstained from pleasures such as wine and grooming his hair. If the Torah considers it a sin to abstain from treating your body to comforts such as wine and grooming, so much more so is it sinful for one to abstain from all the other pleasures of life."
>
> **ঙ৺ Babylonian Talmud, *Ta'anit* 11a**

And so, like a famished panther, I stalked the Sundance and The Stage Stop almost nightly in search of prey, salivating at the sight of any entity remotely resembling or smacking of the feminine. I was getting desperate. Inside my sacks, the sperm count was swelling to an all-time high, and the overpopulation was driving me into a frenzy. I'm not being honest here. That's macho talk. I was simply longing for intimacy, some closeness, the warmth of someone's breath other than that of the guy seated next to me on the bar stool blabbering and blubbering about his guilt over killing coyote pups on behalf of ranchers who felt their livestock threatened. The warm breath I envisioned was more like that of the attractive blonde woman behind the bar with the tatoo above her left breast, or the woman seated two tables away with beautiful Celtic green eyes and the lips of a nymph. Or the sleeveless woman with the long brown hair playing pool in the dark recesses of the room, the biceps of her supple, sensuous arms flexing each time she sent the cue ball rolling.

But all these ladies were taken. None left for the horny runaway renegade rabbi hiding out in Gentile country while down in Boulder wild Jewish women were swooning and moaning in their longing for him.

> Oh, at night when I'm a feelin' blue and lonely,
> I weave in and out of ever' bar in town,
> But ever'body's settin' with another,
> Ever'body's turnin' me down
> Once I met a woman warm and friendly
> Sippin' on tequila all alone.
> We got to talkin' and I never felt so happy,
> But then her husband came along and took her home.
>
> Another time I saw this woman writing
> Her tender fingers didn't wear a ring.
> But then she posted up the note that she had written.
> It said: "Lost, a brand new golden wedding ring."
>
> I asked one girl if she was free to date me.
> To my surprise she smiled and said she can.
> Then she said she needed two more operations
> 'Cuz up until last week she was a man.
>
> Oh, ever' woman's got a ring on her finger.
> There don't seem to be no finger left fer me.
> Ever'body seems to be taken,
> There don't seem to be nobody left fer me.

✍ Song: 1987

The historical novel was at a standstill. I could not bring myself to write such a holy book while the Evil Inclination was seated smack in the middle of my cabin introducing one lewd thought after another

as I struggled desperately to keep my mind off of sex and to concentrate instead on writing. I couldn't figure it out. I had done the
righteous thing by not misleading the Boulderites or myself and
instead moving back into the mountains. Where did I go wrong in
doing right? Was it my association with saloon life and rowdies? Was
it my isolation from the Jewish community and from teaching with
wholeheartedness? Had Jonah fled his calling once more after it had
felt safe to do so again? Could the Rockies flood? Was I asleep again?
Was I spiritually absent while deceiving myself that I was more present and fulfilled than ever? Had I come to a standstill? Is this the life
I wanted?

(AP/UPI)—A reclusive 112-year-old Colorado mountain
man was found dead in his primitive cabin yesterday
clutching onto a photograph of a sleevelesss woman
playing pool. The man was identified as a former rabbi
who had fled his calling some eighty years ago to make
his living singing songs for beer. A shed full of six-
pack cartons was discovered behind the cabin as well
as a stack of outdated Hebrew calendars and a box of
mildewing matzoh. His body was claimed this morning
by the Sisterhood of the Boulder Jewish Community.

I rose from the creaky wooden chair, pulled the paper out of the
typewriter and crumpled it. It felt sacrilegious even for a sacrilegious
guy like me to be writing this holy woman's story while living an
unholy lifestyle. I paced the room of the one-room cabin, scheming
against the Evil Inclination as he sat there glibly perched atop the
pot belly stove scheming against me.

I walked over to the window and gazed blankly out at the tall
pine trees blanketing the rising slope behind the cabin. My weaker
eye (the one on the right) was drawn to a particularly thick, old tree
about a hundred yards away. Seated beneath the sluggish branches

of the ancient growth was the first century B.C.E. Hillel the Elder teaching a circle of women and men, gesturing with his hands, laughing, getting serious, then chuckling, pointing upward, then downward, then to his heart, then outward. I flung open the window to hear what he was saying: "So, again—in a situation where no one is doing what needs to be done, *you* do it!!" (Babylonian Talmud, *Avot* 2:4). He then looked up and pointed straight at me.

———————

I shut the window, walked straight up to the Evil One, and looked him right in the eye.

"Okay, old friend, I'm taking a stand. I'm gonna make some changes around here starting now."

He laughed. "Seems to me that that's about all you've been doing these past few years: making changes. One change after another. Fits your name perfectly: ger-shon, 'ever-changing sojourner.'"

"No, really, it's gonna be different from now on. First, I'm gonna find me a cabin really really really remote, where I can be nurtured once more by Nature's call ... "

"You mean a place with plumbing?"

"Very funny."

"You really think you'll be less horny somewhere else than here?"

"I think I will be less prone to it if I just make some kind of move in my life, in any which direction, and making a physical move is going to help that along. Like Hillel the Elder said: 'In a situation where ...'"

"I know what the old man said, but still you're only wasting your time. You need to go to back to Boulder to be with the community. And there, my young friend, you will also find all the intimacy you ever dreamed of."

"Life is bigger than intimacy, Evil One. I need to start here in my heart, not down there in my pupick."

"You're gonna end up with blueballs."

"No such thing."

"Is, too."

"Is not."

"Is, too."

"Is not."

I took a stand. First I quit the ranch work so I could have more time to write without passing out from fatigue. Then I found a few odd jobs to do thanks to this bloodshot-eyed guy named David something who farmed out menial labor to wandering freelancers and freeloaders like myself. His take was a modest two bucks per my hourly eight dollars. Still missing in my campaign toward personal transformation was relocation to a more remote setting.

So one night, I went to The Stage Stop to ask around again. I slid up on a barstool beside a big burly bearded guy with a pearl-handled revolver nestled deep in a worn, leather holster. He was swallowing one mug of beer after another while busily mumbling Jew jokes to the man on his left. I didn't pick up the punchline too clearly because of the noise in the saloon, but there was something in there about pizzas, Jews, and ovens. Like a really bad anti-Semitic Joke. Ignoring the Hittite and instead concentrating on the tattoo above the left breast of Carol, the attractive blonde woman behind the bar, I asked her whether she knew of any really remote cabins for rent somewhere deep deep in the woods.

"Well," she shouted above the noise while pouring the fifteenth beer for the Hittite, "my husband's got this old cabin in the woods he rents out sometimes. It's pretty isolated. No neighbors, no plumbing, got wood heat, but you can't drive to it. Gotta park on the road and hike a bit."

"Wow! That describes the cabin I'm looking for. Who's your husband? Is he here? Can I call him? Can I leave you a number where I pick up my messages? Does he ever hang at the Stage?"

"He's sittin' right next to ya."

There was a pause for what seemed to be a long period of time. I looked to my right. Nothing but the door to the urinals. To my left: the Hittite.

"Him? This guy? This is your husband? Are you sure?"

"Yup. That's my Carter. Right next to ya. Yer in luck! I can recognize Carter any time any where. A beer in one hand, a cigarette in
the other."

I felt the growing sensations of my dormant Jewishness, unveiled
abruptly by the stark contrast of the Jew-bashing Hittite beside me.
Not knowing what to do next, I just sat still for a while, quietly sip-
ping my brandy. In the mirror behind the bar in front of me I saw
a clouded reflection of myself in full Hasidic regalia, long black coat,
wide-brimmed black hat, long sidelocks, long beard, nursing a shot
of borscht on the rocks with a prune juice chaser, a humongous volume of the Talmud spread out in front of me to folio 57b of the tractate of *Gitin:*

> Some of the descendants of the evil Haman (357 B.C.E.),
> who sought to wipe us out, actually became saintly
> rabbis who taught Torah in Israel. And some of the
> descendants of the wicked King Sanchariv (548 B.C.E.),
> who displaced our people and destroyed many of us and
> much of our land, actually became some of the greatest
> of our spiritual masters. And who were they? Sh'mayya
> and Av'tal'yon, the teachers of Hillel the Elder.

Slowly, I turned toward the Hittite, whose descendants would
possibly become among the greats of my people, and tapped him
gently on his right shoulder. He turned around to face me, his eyes
bloodshot with racial jokes, his beard speckled with glowing embers
of cigarette ashes.

"Ugggh."

"You Carter?" I shouted in a Yiddish accent while stroking my
beard in a rabbinic way, swaying to and fro as if studying Talmud
or praying.

"Uggggh."

"De name's Vinkler. Ger'shen Vinkler. You hef ah pretty vife over
der, mit der tatoo over der by de breast over der."

"Uggggh."

"She told me, yur vife, dot maybe you got for me ah cabin in der voods over der some ver. Nu?"

"Ugggh."

"I see. Un for how much you gonna rent it, if you don't mind mine asking?"

"Uggggh."

"Ah hundred dollars? Dis is good. Nu, vhen cun I see it, der cabin?"

"Uggggggh."

"Gut. I meet you outside der Stage Stop tomorrow at twelv. Good. Nu. So. It vas ver'a nice to talking mit you. Cun I buy you maybe ah shot of borscht? Hah? No? Hokay, so it's no. Not ah problem. T'anks. You can go beck now to der jokes about Jews, you *schmutz*."

Of course that isn't exactly how the conversation went, but it's kind of how it sounded to me, you know: the felt sense of it. I mean, it is really funny how anti-Semitism brings out one's Jewish identity. Even if you're not Jewish. Amazing stuff.

Next afternoon I found myself bouncing about in the back of an old half-ton pick-up with wheels so out of alignment I swear the truck was driving sideways. We pulled up to the edge of a rushing creek winding its way around the foot of a heavily treed slope. Carter headed up the slope with Carol and myself in tow. We came to a narrow trail and followed it a while to a small cabin with a screened-in porch nestled amid a thicket of aromatic pine trees. It was perfect.

"Uggggh."

"Pardon me?"

"Uggggh."

"That's what I thought you said. The answer is: Wow. It's perfect."

"Uggggggh."

"That's not a problem. I can build one, or maybe just buy a portable chemical toilet."

"Uggggh?"

"Yes. I'll take it. But not for a hundred. I gotta give you at least one twenty-five."

"Ugggh."

"No, I insist. One twenty-five. Heck. Make it one fifty and we'll call it even."

"Uggggh."

"Listen I know I drive a hard bargain, my friend, but I'm not taking this gem for less than one fifty."

"Uggggh.

"Okay, okay. One twenty-five it is. A deal!"

Carter grew to like me. Within the week, he came climbing up that slope schlepping a fifty-five gallon drum that he transformed into a powerful heating stove to replace the real one. That drum got so hot during the ensuing winter moons that I often had to run outside to cool off.

It wasn't long before Carter discovered from acquaintances at the Sundance that I wrote songs. So one night, while stopping off at The Stage Stop to have a … uh … to pay the rent, he asked me why I didn't sing any of my songs at The Stage Stop. I told him it's too noisy, and that it wasn't set up for performances. He then shouted in my ear: "Uggghhh!" Translation: "Write me a song about money, and then you can sing it here."

Eager to make damn sure that great rabbis would one day emerge from the loins of this giant white supremacist biker, I quickly composed a song about money and drove straight to The Stage Stop the night I finished writing it. Carter climbed up on a table full of beer bottles and shot a round into the air. Everyone ducked. (Turned out to be a blank). The saloon became as quiet as the Judean desert. He then announced that I would sing a song I'd written for him, and that anyone who made any noise during the song would have to wait a long while before they'd ever be able to speak again. It was stone cold silent as I positioned my guitar while Carter squatted on the table and held the lyrics in front of my eyes. It was my first captive audience.

Cowboys and Hittites

Some folks say you can't live without money,
Y'gotta hang on to ever' little bit.
Yeah, some folks say you ain't nothin' without money,
But I say money ain't it.

Got nothin' in my drawers, nothin' in my pockets,
Got no electricity runnin' through my sockets,
Got my clothes on my back, but nothin' in the closets,
Got a whole lotta coupons, and bottles for deposits.

I know a whole lotta folks who got a whole lotta money,
But they look a lot sadder than me,
And here I am with holes in my pockets
Feelin' filthy rich just to be.

Got nothin' in my drawers, nothin' in my pockets,
Got no electricity runnin' through my sockets,
Got my clothes on my back, but nothin' in the closets,
Got a whole lotta coupons, and bottles for deposits,

Got me a friend, he owns ten acres,
But it cost him a helluva lotta bread,
And here I am in the National Forest
On a one hundred thousand acre spread.

Got nothin' in my drawers, nothin' in my pockets,
Got no electricity runnin' through my sockets,
Got my clothes on my back, but nothin' in the closets,
Got a whole lotta coupons, and bottles for deposits.

🎜 Song: 1987

Then one night, as I stopped in to pay the rent, Carter sat on the barstool where he was born and bred, and ignored me completely.

I gave Carol the cash and told her for the fourth time how much I loved that cabin. She wiped some shot glasses and motioned toward Carter with her graceful mane.

"What's with him?" I asked.

"Ask him."

I sat down next to him and ordered a beer. He kept his head turned away, fixing his attention on the cowboy seated to his left. I bought him a beer. Carol put the mug in front of him and told him it was from me. She couldn't pronounce Gershon, so she called me "Gus."

Carter turned to me and mumbled, his fingers playing with the beer mug.

"Ugggh."

"Oh? You're upset with me, aye? About what?"

"Uggggggh."

"You found out what?"

"Ugggggh."

"Oh, that I'm Jewish. Well, yeah. I am Jewish. What of it?"

"Ugggghhh."

"Why didn't I *tell* you? You never *asked*."

"Uggggggh."

"You don't like Jews. Gee, I never would've guessed."

"Uggghhh."

"I see. And here you are renting your cabin to a Jew."

"Ugggghhhh."

"Aha. Pretty pissed about it. I see. Well, uh … Carter, do you mind telling me what it is about Jews you don't like?"

"Ugggghhhhh."

"Aha. Do I seem like that kind of person to you?"

"Uggggh."

"I might be a what?"

"Uggghhh."

"Oh, an exception. Thanks, but have you ever met Jews before? That is, other than myself?"

"Uggghhhh."

"No, eh? So how can you make those judgments about them?"

"Uggghhh."

"Oh, I see. Stuff you have been reading. Well, let me tell you something, Carter, I've read a lot of stuff about your kind of people, too, and then when I actually meet them and relate with them I discover they are as human as I am. I don't go around judging people by what I read about them, or by what other people say about them."

"Ugghhhh."

"We what?"

"Ugghhh."

"We killed Christ? Do you believe in Christ, Carter? Are you a devout Christian?"

"Ugggghhh."

"Yeah, I didn't think so. So what do you care if we killed Christ?"

"Ugghhh"

"Oh, it's the idea of it, that we would kill someone like that. I see. Good point. Only, fact is that Jesus was a Jew, no different than the ones you hate. The majority of the Jews in the world during the time of Jesus didn't even live in the Land of Israel, let alone Jerusalem, and had never heard of him. And anyway, why would we want to kill him? There was nothing about him that would warrant that. The whole story is a bunch of bunk invented by later writers to ally the then fledgling Christian movement with Roman sentiment toward the Jews. You're gonna buy that crap? Jesus was one of us. We had no reason to get rid of him. The Romans and their collaborators in our Temple had plenty reason because they were paranoid around rabble-rousers like him who threatened not the religious status-quo but the *political* status quo. Read some first-century history, Carter, then come back and hate us."

"Ugggghhh."

"Really? Bankers? Know any Jewish bankers? I could sure use a loan."

"Uggghh."

"And the Jews run *what?*"

"Uggghhhh."

"Oh, Hollywood. Aha. Funny. No one in the communities I grew up knew anyone in Hollywood. Besides, do you enjoy going to the movies? Renting videos?"

"Ugghhh."

"If we're running Hollywood, Carter, you ought to be grateful to us or you would have nothing to watch but black and white newsreels of World War One and a handful of Daffy Duck reruns."

He grabbed the beer I'd bought him and guzzled it down without coming up for air. Then he looked at me, looked at his empty mug, then back at me, then at Carol. There was a pause for what seemed to be a long period of time. Carter bought me a beer. We continued dialoguing and alternately buying each other beers for what seemed like hours. In the end, I couldn't walk straight, so he helped me to his truck and drove me to his place where I spent the night on a sofa peppered with anti-Semitic cigarette burns.

We have been close friends ever since.

Years later, after I'd left Colorado, he wrote me a letter, completely misspelled. At the bottom, Carol added the following: "Gus, I want you to know that Carter has never in his life sat his ass down to write a letter to anyone."

Chapter Thirteen

Attack of the Zalman

I had no phone out there in the sticks, so I registered with an answering service in Boulder, and I'd call in daily in case there was a family emergency, or I won something. Lately, though, I kept getting this cryptic message from an elder sounding guy with a kind of Austrian accent who identified himself only as "Zalman" and who kept insisting that it was important I call him back. Collect. Having no clue who this *nudnik* was, I ignored his messages. After two weeks of ignoring his phone attempts I now began receiving notes from him, brief letters, about three of them:

> Gersh, call me, please.
>
> We have some very important things to discuss.
>
> Call collect.

Wow. This guy, whoever he was, sure was persistent. But so was I. I had no idea who this man was and what he wanted, and had no intentions of responding just because someone decided to throw a ball my way. Maybe, I thought, maybe if I ignored him long enough, he would give up and go away.

Not. In the next note, I noticed his full name in the letterhead that carried his message: Rabbi Zalman Schachter-Shalomi. The name was somewhat familiar. Zalman Schachter, Zalman Schachter, Zalman Schachter ... ah, yes, the crazy sixty-something-year-old guru rabbi. What in the hell did he want with *me?*

Years earlier, during my Orthodox paradigm, I had once experienced a very brief encounter with this, this eccentric chief rabbi of the Hippies and the Yippies, this overgrown flower child who was busily frolicking in the Nirvana of the Sexual Revolution and other psychedelicacies while I was poring over the holy books and living a devout life, and missing all of it. What the heck did he want from me? That brief encounter, I recalled, had been a real turn-off to me back then. As an outreach rabbi for the ultra-Orthodox, I was sent to Toronto to attend the International Jewish Student Network Conference. Among other tasks there, I was supposed to familiarize myself with what other outreach groups were doing, and to introduce others to my successful work with the coffee house program. Someone had then mentioned this wild crazy guy, Rabbi Zalman Schachter, and that I ought to see what heretical insanity he was perpetrating. So I went to the room where he was doing his workshop, opened the door ever so cautiously, peeked in, and left instantly in disgust. My God. You would never believe what I saw! There, in a circle of people, stood Rabbi Schachter draped in prayer shawl and philacteries while holding hands with women and men huddled in a circle together, swaying in ecstatic prayer. How disgusting. How sacrilegious. How blasphemous.

So now this heretic wants to connect with *me?* With the pure, holy Gershon Winkler? Never. And, anyway, what for?

I threw his letter into the fire and went to sleep.

The next morning I went to work nearby building a horse fence for a nice couple. Kathy supervised me as I dug post holes, while her long-time live-in boyfriend, Harry, was in Denver working for some investment firm. Now, now, I know what you're thinking. But you're dead wrong, and how dare you, the reader, allow yourself to become so glibly presumptious about me and assume that I hit on this woman. She was happily involved with Harry and needed me like a leopard needed corn flakes. She was real nice to me and fed me berries while I worked.

After I'd finished the horse fence, she hired me to dig a major ditch around the house so they could build a patio there. So daily I worked in her presence digging and digging and digging while she measured the depth. Then she would gently ask me to dig deeper. As the days wore on, she would quiz me about my life because, as she explained, somehow I didn't seem to her the laborer type. So I told her about my life as a rabbi and the shift I chose to make in my lifestyle.

GERSHON WINKLER
1949–1987

He chose dirt over Torah.

Turned out that her boyfriend, Harry, too, was Jewish. A nice Jewish boy from Brooklyn who spent some years in yeshiva and then chucked it all for life in the Colorado Rockies with his Episcopalian girlfriend. One afternoon, as I was standing chest-deep in the nearly completed ditch, a jeep pulls up and Harry appears. Standing tall and shading me from the sun he gives me his hand and greets me with the traditional "*Shalom Aleichem.*" I greeted him back with the traditional "*Aleichem Shalom.*"

"So," he says, "Kathy tells me that there's a rabbi in my ditch."

"Yeah, I know. I've been trying for over a week now to dig him up."

Harry laughed and climbed down into the ditch. He took the shovel from me and took a turn at digging where I'd left off, while engaging me in lively, friendly conversation about *yeshiva*, about

New York, doing Jewish in the rurals, and plans for the patio. He admitted his continued puzzlement over what the hell a runaway rabbi was doing digging ditches at six dollars an hour.

"You're right. I should be charging seven-fifty."

"No, I mean you could be a rabbi for some huge synagogue in some big city making ninety grand a year plus benefits. I mean, you're an author, for gossake."

"We were once a rural people, you know," I said, climbing out of the ditch, "and rabbis earned their livelihood digging ditches, farming, herding goats, and mending sandals. I'm just following tradition, Harry."

Kathy came out and invited me to stay for supper. It was the first home cooked meal I'd had in many months. Maybe even a year. I accepted. We became good friends and they kept me busy, soon weaning me off of my middle-man so that I could keep the full eight bucks an hour all to myself.

Behind their generous backs I continued feeding David what's-his-name his commission. After all, he had been the one who'd gotten me the work. The principles of Talmudic law and ethics still burned fiercely in my yarmulka-less heart. You know the old adage: You can take the Jew out of the Torah, but you can't take the Torah out of the Jew.

After dinner I asked Harry if I could use the phone. I felt inspired meeting a fellow Jewish fugitive from Brooklyn hiding out in the Rockies. The delicious home-cooked meal helped, too.

"Yes, operator, we will accept the charges. Thank you. Good afternoon, B'nai-Or Religious Fellowship, this is Leah, can I help you?"

"Um, uh, is Rabbi Schachter there?"

"I'll check. Who should I say is calling, please?"

"Gershon Winkler retur ... "

"Rabbi Winkler?! Oh, please don't hang up! He will be right with you! Omigosh!"

Pause.

"Hello, Gersh? Listen, I am so glad you called. I thought it would maybe take the Jaws of Life to get you to return my call. Listen, you and I have got to talk. I assume you visit your family in New York from time to time. Can you stop by in Philadelphia so we can meet? Listen to what I tell you. I will send you a plane ticket. Come early next week. We need to talk. This is very important."

Click.

"Rabbi Scha ... hello? Hello! Hello?"

Dial tone.

I hung up the phone feeling like some kind of secret agent who'd just received word of his next assignment from headquarters. My head was spinning. I sat down on a kitchen stool to regain my composure and then headed home. I had finally given in to the madman and called him collect. What was I getting myself into? All I knew was that a plane ticket was en-route to the post office in Pineview, and that I was going to see my kids barely two weeks after I'd just seen them. And that I was then going to be on a train from New York to Philadelphia to meet this pestering guru and hopefully get him off my back for good.

I slept deeply that night and dreamed of the *sefirot*, the ten spirals of divine emanation often referred to in the Kabbalah. I had no idea of what I was getting myself into next. Neither did the Evil Inclination who stayed up all that night piecing together the charred remains of Zalman's cryptic letters and phone messages.

A week and a half later I found myself on the platform of a train station in the Germantown area of Philadelphia. It was close to ten at night and there wasn't a soul in sight other than this older guy wandering around the platform waiting for someone. I looked up and down the platform wondering where the disciples were, the groupies of Guru Schachter who I assumed would have been dispatched by the great master to pick me up. Not a one. Just this older guy pacing up and down the dimly lit platform, sporting a well-worn beret and stroking his grey beard now and then.

"Reb Gershon?"

"Reb Zalman?"

We shook hands, two rabbis neither of whom was dressed like one, each looking for someone who looked somewhat like a rabbi. He escorted me downstairs to what I presumed would be his late model limo. I mean, we're talking about a guy who's got followers all over the world. He ushered me to a tiny illegally parked Fiat so faded I couldn't make out the color. I got in beside him amid a rubble of papers, cassettes, brochures, and books. I'd have guessed he was a peddler if I didn't know better. Names of God were flying all about the windshield, suspended from the rear-view mirror by crystal woven strings. The prayer for journeying was pasted crooked on the dashboard half-covered by coffee stains painted by sudden stops during caffeine fixes.

"What's all this?" I asked, pointing at the God Names along the windshield.

"That's in case, you know, that God forbid there's a fatal accident, I would want that the last thing I see is the Name of God."

"What for? You'll see God Itself at that point. Screw the names."

"It goes like this, Gersh: At the last moment, if God forbid something should happen, my last words are likely to be: 'Shit! Fuck!' But if the last thing I see is the God Names, I will go out in a more, you know, pure way, with the name of God on my lips."

"As in 'Goddamit'?"

He laughed so hard we almost collided with a trolley. "Not now, Gersh," he begged, "not now."

We arrived at a big house resembling the set from the movie "The Addams Family" and he turned off the car. As we ascended the old stone steps to the house I could still hear the engine sputtering.

"Does your car always recite the God Names every time you turn it off?"

He laughed. "Not now, Gersh," he begged, "please, not now."

Turned out Zalman enjoyed my humor a great deal, only not just now. It was never the right time. Too much to talk about, too much to get done. Life was short. The world was standing on the verge of a major paradigm shift and I was cracking jokes.

Inside his deeply lived-in living room he bid me to find a comfortable place to sit, which took me a while as most of the sitting spaces were blanketed by a myriad of thousands of years of ancient and medieval Aramaic and Hebraic texts. He disappeared into the kitchen while I melted into a vacant spot on a sofa probably built long before the advent of springs. From the kitchen he called to me, asking if I was hungry. I was about to say Yes when he yelled something about making me some scrambled eggs.

> And it shall come to pass
>
> that before they have even called,
>
> I shall have already answered;
>
> before they have even spoken,
>
> I shall have already heard.
>
> **Isaiah 65:24**

"Gersh!"

"Yeah!"

"You like your eggs scrambled or over easy?"

I hadn't a clue what "over easy" meant. Five years was hardly enough time to acculturate a yeshiva boy in the ways of the nations and their menu jargon.

"Scrambled is fine!"

"Gersh!"

"Yeah!"

"Do you smoke?"

"No!"

"You know which smoke I'm talking about?"

"No!"

"Never mind. Do you want some juice?!"

"Sure! Thanks!"

"We have apple, cranberry, and orange!"

"Orange!"

I couldn't believe it. It was nearing eleven o'clock in the evening and I was being served breakfast by a guru with no servants at his beckon, a master with no disciples in waiting. Maybe Jewish gurus were different than most other gurus, I figured. After all, the ancient gurus of my people, whose followings far exceeded those of Reb Zalman, refused to take anything from the people, not so much as a donkey.

> Not a single donkey have I ever
> taken from any one of them.
>
> **◄ई Numbers 16:15**

> Have I ever taken from any of you
> so much as a donkey or an ox?
>
> **◄ई 1 Samuel 12:3**

The eggs were badly charred but tasted fair with a lot of ketchup and orange juice. I assumed that the master would join me at the table. Instead, he slipped on his jacket, grabbed his car keys, and headed for the door.

"Gersh. I have to run. Do you mind babysitting a little while? I'll be right back."

"You have a baby?"

"There are three kids. They're sleeping upstairs. I'll be right back."

Thus my initial encounter with Reb Zalman.

The following morning I found myself seated beside the master in his Fiat again as we drove all over the city on a wide variety of errands. First we dropped his youngest, Yotam, at a preschool place. Then we sped out to the suburbs to pick up a bathing suit that his daughter Shalvi had forgotten at Day Camp. Then we headed back to the business section of town so Zalman could up his optical prescription by one point to ease his work in front of the computer screen.

As he drove frantically through the maze of city streets and traffic, he slapped a clipboard on my lap and instructed me to take notes as he distilled thousands of years of kabbalistic wisdom into a fresh bottle of paradigm shift. I had no idea what he was talking about, but it sounded good, actually refreshing, and in some deep way awakened my own dormant theology for my own personal paradigm shift. This guy, I realized, had taken daring jumps similar to mine, although it was clear to me that he'd had a parachute on him when he went through his transformations from Orthodoxy to Flexidoxy.

We stopped at virtually every optical store in Philadelphia, double-parked, or parked in front of fire hydrants and driveways—whatever it took. My job was to sit in the car and look out for the police while Zalman rushed inside to try and convince the opticians to upgrade his lenses by a single point. I couldn't figure out why he kept coming back out frustrated, and why we were hopping from one store to another, until we found a legal parking space, which enabled me to join him inside.

"I need these lenses moved up a point."

"Do you have a prescription for your request, sir?"

"No, I don't, but I know exactly what I need, just one point stronger."

"I'm sorry, sir, but we need a prescription."

"Listen, I don't have time to sit in the doctor's office waiting for a prescription. Couldn't you just give me lenses with one point stronger than these? Just one point. I know what I need."

"We're sorry, sir, but we can't do that without a prescription."

"I will take full responsibility. Just one point."

"Sorry, sir. Can't do."

"Can I see the manager?"

"I am the manager."

As we got back in the car, my mind wandered off to The Stage Stop, to Kathy and Harry's ditch, to my cabin in the Rockies, to Carol and Carter. What the hell was I doing hanging out with this madman amid this endless metropolis? I wanted to go home. This was maddening. Paradigm shift or no paradigm shift, this was not my world and I wanted out of there pronto.

Three stores later he found an optician who agreed to do it for him. We could now proceed to the office of his organization, B'nai-Or. Inside the B'nai-Or office, two women were busily getting a mailing out. The master joined them and before I knew what was happening I, too, was affixing labels on thousands of envelopes.

"Well, Zalman, I now know why you were so eager to get me out here. There are only three of you trying to get this mailing out."

"Not now, Gersh," he begged, chuckling.

"Look at how the women are getting their labels on straight," I observed at one point, "and look at ours, all crooked, all over the envelopes. Amazing."

"That's because women are durative, men are punctive."

"Oh."

Eventually, we were seated alone in his study and he explained to me why he had wanted to meet me. Well, he *almost* began to explain when he suddenly wanted to show me something on the computer instead. He turned to the screen and tapped at the keyboard with the same intensity he had exhibited running in and out of optical establishments.

"Look at this."

I looked. It was a poetic translation of a traditional prayer. He continued showing me a lot of his writings, then slapped a half a dozen cassettes of his talks into my arms, which I hid under books and papers as we left the study to find a quieter place to talk. Finally, he explained that he'd read some of my books, liked my writing, and wanted me to move east and transcribe his teachings into a book. Someone had put up a grant for this project, he explained, and he felt from what he'd heard about me from the Aquarians and the Boulderites, and from what he'd read of my works, that I was the best candidate for the job. I was not only a good writer, he explained, but also had the background in traditional Jewish learning necessary to more clearly articulate his teachings around the paradigm shift.

"What's a paradigm shift?" I asked.

He laughed, assuming I was joking. "Not now, Gersh, please, not now."

"I think I understand." Unbeknownst to him I truly got what a paradigm shift was all about: Not now.

"It would pay $350 a week," he continued, "for five years."

"Wow. That's a lot. And a steady income, yet. Wow"

"But you'd have to move out here, of course, so we can *schmooze* as we write the book."

"The money is very tempting, Reb Zalman, and so is the security of a regular income. And I love writing and all. But, I can't live in the city. I need to be in Nature."

"Listen, Gersh, there's a very large heavily wooded park right nearby, with streams, and a river ..."

"Can't do it. A nearby park is nice. But I need to live in the country. I'm sure I could find a cabin to rent out here, but it won't be in or near the city."

"Okay. But not further than 35 miles or so. Because we have to meet regularly."

"Deal."

Within a month I was out of Colorado and cruising the countryside of eastern Pennsylvania within a 35-40 mile radius of Philadelphia. With no luck. Firstly, it wasn't nearly rural enough. Secondly, it was expensive. So, being the boundary-crosser that I am, I ventured beyond the agreed-upon radius, to 45 miles, then 50, then 55, then 60, then 65—Bingo! Rurals. Woods. Remoteness. Amish country. Cheap secluded cabin rentals. Even got me a job doing the early morning shift on a small, family-operated dairy farm to stay in shape.

The commutes to Philadelphia didn't turn out to be as frequent as I thought they would be, probably because I had no chance to shower between the time my shift at the farm ended and the time I was supposed to meet with Zalman. Sometimes I was in such a hurry to get to the meetings that I'd have to scrub the cow shit off my boots on the steps of the B'nai-Or office. When I arrived for my meetings, the secretaries often split for extended lunch periods, and the executive director, I noticed, ordered a case of Lysol spray. Soon the office was swarming with horse flies, a phenomena that was otherwise unknown in urban Philadelphia since the introduction of the automobile.

Zalman wasn't too happy with my writing at first because I made the book reflect too much how he actually spoke, a style I found colorful and fun. Instead he wanted me to write in the way I had written *my* books. Then, after showing him a chapter written in my *own* style he complained that it didn't sound enough like *him.* So I struggled to find a middle way.

Besides trying to write books, the master was often called to lecture or do weekend seminars on Jewish mysticism across the country. On one such gig, he asked me to go with him.

"Zalman, I'm not really into teaching anymore. So no thanks."

"Gersh, I'll do all the teaching. You just come as my aide. I need someone to help me *schlep* the projector, the laptop, the books, and so on."

"Okay. I'll do that."

So we flew to Chicago where Zalman taught at the Oasis center and I served as his logistics assistant.

I was soon to realize how blind I had been to this scheming, conniving coyote who had never intended for me to write some damn book, but to come out of the mountains and teach the people again. He had long ago eyed me, long ago watched my process, long ago waited for an opportunity to lure me out of my hermitage so that he could get my feet wet again and harmonize the rabbi within me with my recent paradigm shift. That sonofagun. Because, smack in the middle of teaching from the wisdom of the eighteenth-century Rabbi Nachmon of Breslav, Zalman handed me the book in front of a hundred seekers and asked me to continue translating the text while he disappeared to the bathroom. His "visit" to the bathroom lasted well over an hour, leaving me with the unforeseen task of teaching from a book I'd never really paid much attention to. But Rabbi Nachmon's wisdom shook loose a lot of tangled stuff inside of me and freed up a lot of ambivalence around myself as a spiritual teacher capable of interpreting the ancient wisdom in contemporary verbiage, and from the place where I was at in my personal unfolding.

> "The place where you
> are standing is holy."
>
> **Exodus 3:5**

> And God heard the cry of the
> young man where he was at.
>
> **Genesis 21:17**

When the weekend was over, the Jews in the group begged Zalman for more. They decided on the spot to form their own little *havurah*, or fellowship, that would meet monthly in someone's home and continue the studies and practices that Zalman had introduced to them. Would he, they asked, visit them monthly until they got off the ground? He would, of course, but because he was so much in demand, the group realized they couldn't afford him. The next best thing, he advised them, was the cheaper option: me. And so, for the next three years, this group would fly me to Chicago for a weekend of teaching, at a thousand bucks a shot.

To this day, I don't think Zalman knows that I lived 63 miles out of Philadelphia that year. That's right. It was only one year. Because by year's end, the grant donor decided to redirect the money elsewhere. And suddenly I found myself out of a job, no income, stranded in the remotes of the western portion of eastern Pennsylvania.

Chapter Fourteen

Back to the Backwoods

I left Pennsylvania.

I drove west on the turnpike, intending to start anew perhaps on some ranch in, say, Wyoming. Based on the map, it was one of the least populated states in the union, with only half a million people in the entire state. There, I would find lots of wide open spaces, lots of wilderness, all the "Nature" and seclusion I wanted. Wyoming it is!

Crossing into Ohio, I drove past a sign indicating that if, on the other hand, I'd consider returning to West Virginia, the next exit would lead me there.

No way. My mind was made up. I was going to Wyoming. I mean, West Virginia was also very rural, and did have the advantage of being only eight hours from the kids as opposed to the three days it would take to drive from Wyoming to New York, or the expensive airfare to fly from there. I pulled off the exit onto Route 7 and parked alongside the road. It would be nice, I surmised, to be more accessible to the kids as I had been during my sojourn in Pennsylvania, or when I was living in West Virginia. Maybe I should be mature about this and put off my preference for the wild west until the kids are finished with high school.

I drove down the road toward West Virginia.

On the other hand, I was really psyched up about going to Wyoming and breaking fresh ground. The challenge of it felt exhilarating. Wyoming.

I made a U-Turn and headed back toward the westbound exit of the Turnpike.

But then again, what could be more important than my daughters. To suddenly disrupt the momentum of visiting with them every two weekends or so would be one more slap in their faces added to the divorce. What kind of father was I to put my personal fantasies ahead of my children?

I made a U-Turn and headed south toward West Virginia.

On the other hand, which is better for them? An 85% happy father living in closer proximity, or a 150% happy father living where he truly felt he wanted to be, albeit farther away?

I made a U-Turn and headed north toward the Turnpike.

Aha! Of course! It was the Evil Inclination again, trying to talk me into selfish pursuits to the neglect of the needs of my teenage daughters who would greatly benefit from the continuity of the momentum with which I'd been visiting them lately. I will not surrender to that sonofabitch!

I made a U-Turn and headed south toward West Virginia.

All this time, several elderly gentlemen had slowly gathered on the front porch of a small grocery store to watch the unusual spectacle of a perpetually U-Turning 1966 Rambler, which by this time was running on only four of its otherwise six cylinders. They'd never before seen a sight remotely resembling anything like this. And that, my friends, is what the Chosen People thing is all about. Every people is chosen for something. My people were chosen by God to upset the status-quo of things, to shake people out of their stupor, to challenge opticians to issue new lenses without prescriptions, to rent cabins from anti-Semites, or to make a dozen U-Turns in a period of eleven minutes within a radius of three miles on a road less-traveled in eastern Ohio, and give the locals something *fresh* to talk about for a change.

I continued driving into western West Virginia and turned eastward toward the more remote region of the Allegheny Mountains. Once I hit the tiny town of Moorefield, I bought the local weekly paper and holed up in a motel while I looked for a place to rent. The following day, I drove out to a very secluded area called

Jenkins Hollow where a local school teacher was trying to rent out a double-wide, fully-furnished, two-bath, three-bedroom mobile home. It was an old model but spacious, luxurious, and nestled in the middle of the woods completely secluded. Plus it had plumbing and electricity!

"Wow. I love it. It's perfect. But I don't know if I can afford a place like this. Out of curiosity, how much are you wanting for the place?"

"One fifty-fah'v."

"I beg your pardon?"

"One fifty-fah'v."

"Oh. Like one fifty-five a week."

"Nossir, one fifty-fah'v a month."

"One fifty-five a month?"

"One fifty-fah'v."

There was a pause for what seemed to be a long period of time. This was too ideal. A big house with all amenities, fully furnished, with plumbing and electricity, two bathrooms, situated on hundreds of secluded acres of forest, with a year-round creek rushing by less than a hundred yards from the house. And the guy only wanted one hundred and fifty-five bucks a month for it.

"Wow. What's the catch?"

"The catch is, you give me one fifty-fah'v a month, and in return you can live here."

"One fifty-five, aye?"

"One fifty-fah'v."

"Any deposit? Security? Two months advance, or something?"

"Nossir. Jes' one fifty-fah'v."

"One fifty-five?"

"One fifty-fah'v."

There was a pause for what seemed to be a long period of time.

"I'll give you two hundred for it."

"One fifty-fah'v."

"One eighty-five."

"One fifty-fah'v."

"Hmmmm. Not willing to bargain, are you?"

"Nossir. It's one fifty-fah'v. No more, no less."

"One fifty-five?"

"One fifty-fah'v."

"By the way, what time do you have?"

"One fifty-fah'v."

Not being so adept at negotiating, I conceded and gave him his rent and moved in.

Good. So I got myself a great living situation in a beautiful spot in the middle of Jenkins Hollow. Now, what was I going to do for a living? Money was running low and I had to send money to Bryna even though she'd remarried. Not nice to expect some other guy, as good-hearted as he was, to support my kids all by himself. And Judaica Press hadn't given me any further money since I hadn't produced so much as a single chapter. And the Chicago folks weren't flying me in to make my first thous ... uh ... to teach Torah until the following moon. And my last two hundred dollars had just gotten circumcised down to forty-five dollars.

But I wasn't worried. If God was in such a good mood so as to give me two bathrooms, for sure God would find me the means to use them.

> He who has what to eat today and
> says "What shall I eat tomorrow,"
> has little faith.
>
> **Babylonian Talmud, *Sotah* 48b**

I checked the six "Help Wanted" ads in the paper I'd bought and found someone who needed a farm hand to come help out four days a week with some sheep and cows at the competitive rate of three dollars an hour plus a generous supply of free eggs, milk, and non-kosher meat. The farmer's wife interviewed me, liked me, and hired me on the spot. I didn't even have to produce my lengthy resume and bibliography. She then showed me the routine and had

me help her in the barn while her husband went to the nearby hamlet of Petersburg to buy chicken mesh. The woman was very sweet
and good-looking and not happy in her marriage. She observed how
compassionately I sat there listening to her and asked me if it would
be all right if I held her a little. I looked up at the ceiling of the barn
for divine guidance and instead saw the Evil Inclination perched
quite comfortably on one of the rafters with a mischievous smirk on
his face.

───────────

"You gotta be kidding," I said to him in my mind.

"No. I'm not. Go for it. It's been a long time. You've been so good.
You deserve a little intimacy."

"Bullshit. This is bad news and you know it. This is a married woman."

"True. But an unhappily married woman. Have you already forgotten
the teaching in the Talmud about unhappy women?"

───────────

It is written: "And he named his wife *chavvah*,
for she is Mother of all Life" (Genesis 3:20).
This teaches us that woman was meant for aliveness,
certainly not for suffering.

⁌ Babylonian Talmud, *Ketuvot* 61a

"Okay, then," I said to the Evil One, girding my loins, "but only
a platonic, caring hug, understand? And no more."

"Suit yourself."

I got up, walked over to her, and took her in my arms. My entire
midsection burst into flames instantly as I felt the warmth of her
bosom press against my chest through my t-shirt. I tried everything
I could think of to distract my starving libido, but to no avail. I tried
thinking of medieval rabbis, then I tried imaging Moses coming down
North Fork Mountain and throwing the tablets at me, but they flew
right over my head and crash landed behind me against an anti-
quated wooden sled parked in the corner of the barn. I was still on

fire and the Evil Inclination was slapping his thighs in uncontrollable laughter.

"Ooooh," she moaned, "you feel so good, so safe. Where do you live?"

"Jenkins Hollow."

"Jenkins what?"

"Jenkins Hollow."

"Oh, you must mean Jenkins *Holler*."

She clung on tight, slowly moving her face upward toward mine while aiming her full and ready lips toward mine.

Great.

Headlines:

Jerusalem Ordained Rabbi Accused of Adultery

I mean, this was pure biblical material, although it had already been done before, as in the story of Joseph and his trials around the wife of *his* employer who wanted his body daily.

> And it happened ... that his master's wife cast her eyes upon Joseph; and she said: "Lie with me." But he refused, and said ... "How can I do this wrongness, and also sin against God?" And it happened, that as she spoke to Joseph day by day, that he did not listen to her to lie with her, or to be with her in any other manner. And it happened on a certain day, when he went into the house to do his chores, and no other man was around, that she caught him by his garment, saying: "Lie with me." And he left his garment in her hand and fled, and got himself out of there. And it happened that when she saw that he had left his garment in her hand, and had run out, that she

called unto the men of the house and spoke with them,
saying: "See how my husband has brought unto us a
Hebrew to mock us; he came in to lie with me, and I
cried out real loud and he fled, leaving his garment with
me." ... And it happened that when his master heard the
words of his wife ... he put him into the prison.

Genesis 39:7-20

I released her gently, finished helping her, and went home. Thank
you, O wise Torah, for keeping me out of the county jail as well as
the morgue. I continued working there for several months and the
woman quickly got the hint that I was not interested in having an
affair with her. Which, of course, was far from the truth. *Certainly* I
wanted to have sex with her, but it felt so wrong.

A Jew should never claim: "It is against my nature to eat
pork," ... or: "It is against my nature to engage in illicit
sex." Rather, he should declare: "It is within my nature
to eat pork...and it is within my nature to engage in
illicit sex, but what can I do when my Father Who art in
Heaven decreed against it?"

Midrash Sif'ra, K'doshim 9:12

It was extremely difficult for me not to seize the opportunity and
rendezvous with this very willing, attractive woman. But another important piece to it was that I didn't feel any romantic love toward her,
and our connecting would have been totally and exclusively physical
for me, and for her it would offer only temporary, illusory comfort
while further anesthetizing her from dealing with the unresolved discomfort around her marriage. Oh yeah, also it was an immoral thing
to do. But maybe not so immoral since she was not happy with the
guy, and he wasn't treating her right. On the other hand, if that were
the case, she should leave him. But for now she wasn't going to, and

my having an affair with her would only cushion her marital suffering, further delaying her need to bust out of it. On the other hand ...
I voted No.

I went only as far as being someone who would listen to her, while fantasizing how sweet it would be to go to bed with her. The Evil One had failed to put her in my bed, but had succeeded in putting her in my mind.

In some inexplicable way, the experience of *not* going to bed with the farmer's wife had strengthened some limp muscle in me, this time not the *pupick* but the brain and heart muscle. During my periodic visits to the Chicago community, I was often approached by some of the women in the group who wanted to "play" with me. On one occasion a married woman, distressed over her marriage, plain out asked me if I would sleep with her, explaining that she longed so much to make love with a spiritual man. I was very tempted because I was very horny, very flattered, and very attracted to her. Mustering all the strength I could gather, I said to her: "If I went to bed with you, I would be anything but that spiritual man you so long for."

Nevertheless, even though I did not bed the women who wanted me, word spread that I did. This happened after I'd met a woman named Cindy *outside* the context of the community, albeit within Chicago city limits, with whom I *did* become romantically involved in a very deep and serious way. I learned from this episode that as a public figure, I was no longer being seen or judged as is, but rather under an electron microscope.

My romance with Cindy didn't last as long as I'd have wanted it to. I loved her deeply and wanted to spend my life with her, and maybe even a reincarnation or two. At first she felt the same way about me but then realized an hour later that it wasn't as soul deep as she'd originally thought. So she dumped me, but in the gentle, loving way in which I myself had dumped others.

I do admit that I had my eyes on one particular Goddess in that community during those three years of on-and-off teaching in

Chicago, but she completely ignored my intimations of interest in her and never answered my letters.

Back home in my double-wide mansion in the woods, I now resumed writing that historical novel, and slowly, the more I resisted the temptation around the farmer's wife and around the women who wanted my body in Chicago, the more the book was getting written. Then, just when I couldn't take it any more, the farmer's wife's husband asked me to take the truck to Elkins and pick up some bailing wire he couldn't get enough of locally. In Elkins, a bigger sort of town with traffic lights and stuff, I bought a bigger sort of newspaper so that I could look for bigger sorts of job opportunities.

**B'nai B'rith Hillel
Foundation seeks part-time
director for Jewish student
programming at West
Virginia University.**

I went home, updated my resume, and mailed it in. A month went by and I didn't hear from them. Then one day, I got a call. They wanted to interview me. Seems that they had initially dismissed my application because it seemed too unreal: a rabbinic scholar and author holed up in Jenkins Hollow? Probably a fraudulent applicant. But Muriel, the wife of the president of Hillel Foundation, pressed her husband Bennett to re-examine the strange resume and at least meet with me.

West Virginia University was a mere 135 miles west of Jenkins Hollow, so I drove up and down and round and round to the much much much bigger town of Morgantown to interview for the job. The only stipulation I put forth was that I wanted to live in Jenkins Hollow. I refused to relocate to the Morgantown area. I needed to live that remote. They checked me out, studied my resume, and, though still very puzzled as to what in hell a rabbi was doing living way out there, hired me.

I now had income, and my rabbi'ing had swelled from alternate monthly visits to the Chicago group to include also bi-monthly weekend visits to West Virginia University's Jewish student community. There, my programs became so attractive that it drew a great many *not* Jewish students as well, and soon also attracted non-students altogether, entire families, the press, even the Dalai Lama. Okay, maybe he didn't actually show up, but he would have had he been on the mailing list .

Local press coverage about the "circuit-riding rabbi from Jenkins Holler" reached the other side of the walls of the nearby Federal Prison Camp, and soon, at the request of the twenty or so white-collar Jewish inmates from around the country, I was contracted to be their chaplain during the weekends I was in town. Before long, I was also asked by the Feds to visit the Prison Camp for Women in Alderson as well, some 175 miles southeast of Morgantown.

One thing led to another. A volunteer at the women's facility happened to be a Jewish back-to-the-land guy who lived in the woods on his farm, and after meeting me he asked if I'd also visit the small widely scattered Jewish community of Monroe, Greenbrier, and Pocahontas Counties. Then the president of the small Reform Temple in Fairmont asked me to conduct their Sabbath service once a month while I was working in nearby Morgantown.

Within a year I had become a circuit-riding rabbi serving two federal prison camps, a university student organization, and three Jewish communities, across a 435-mile circuit two weekends a month. When the *Wall Street Journal* got wind of this, they sent their Pittsburgh reporter to follow me around and then featured me on the front page with their usual artist's rendition.

I was a rabbi again, and earning a decent livelihood. And somehow, I felt no temptation at the university to hit on any of the young, vulnerable sirens who flocked to my programs. Something was amiss. The Evil Inclination was nowhere to be found. My life was at a standstill, albeit a good one. But the seeming absence of the Evil One had me worried. What was the sonofabitch up to? And would I be prepared?

> Said David to the Holy Blessed One: "The people refer to you as the God of Abraham and the God of Isaac and the God of Jacob. When will they refer to You as the God of David?" Said the Holy Blessed One: "These I tested. You I haven't tested." Said David: "So test me." Said the Holy Blessed One: "Not only will I do as you ask, but I will grant you the advantages that I did not grant to them. I will inform you of the nature of the test and the time of the test. The nature of the test is sexual, and the time of the test is tonight." When David heard this, he spent the entire day making love with his wives in order to be prepared for the evening test, figuring he would be thereby free of any sexual temptation. That evening, having made love to all his wives, he retreated to the roof of the palace for some air, looked across the city, when he saw Bathsheba bathing. Immediately, he sent for her and failed the test. Thus, it has been taught that a tiny organ hangs on the man, and the more he attempts to satisfy it, the hungrier it gets.
>
> ✌ Babylonian Talmud, *Sanhedrin* 107a)

Chapter Fifteen

The Adventures of the Velveteen Rabbi

And it came to pass that the Chicago group fell apart due to the death of a key pillar of the community who had played a major role in holding the group in place. The community decided to fly me out just one more time before they disbanded. The Goddess showed up, too, as I always prayed she would, because each time I taught there I felt very nurtured by her mere presence. Guess it wasn't so mere, after all. Her leg was in a cast that weekend from a knee injury, and I had long ago ceased hinting to her about my interests. I know when to take a hint.

At the end of the weekend, I waited for Paul the host to drive me back to the motel, when the Goddess came over and informed me that she would drive me. Having let go of even the remote possibility of ever getting anywhere with this woman and with the Evil One still in hiding, I told her thanks but Paul was going to drive me. She went over to Paul who was fumbling around looking for his car keys, and told him that she was driving me.

And she did. And we sat in the motel room talking into the wee hours of the morning after which she went home. I was in love. When I got home after an hour flight plus three and a half hours of driving from the airport, I wrote her a brief letter telling her how sweet it was to have spent that time with her.

She wrote back. Ditto.

I wrote back, asking her out on a date.

She wrote back saying, that would be fine, but when? The High Holydays were approaching. Wouldn't I be busy servicing my hefty circuit?

I wrote back, inviting her to do the circuit with me. So, our first date was spent fasting on Yom Kippur while I ran my circuit. It was the least expensive date I ever had. I highly recommend it. In fact, dating during a fast enabled me to relate to her and to see her beyond body stuff, purely in a spirit way. There is no better time to romance someone without the confusion of sexual attraction than on the holy day of Yom Kippur. In fact, that is precisely when Jewish singles got together in ancient times.

> No day was as festive as the fifteenth day of the
> Moon of Av and the holy day of Yom Kippur, for
> then would the single women and men gather in the
> orchards to dance, each bedecked in simple white
> garb so that no one would judge the other based on
> wealth or social station.
>
> **◄§ Babylonian Talmud, *Mishn'nah Ta'anit* 4:8**

A week before my first date with Lakme, I am sitting on the stoop of my mansion, enjoying the scenic view of endless woods, the fragrance of drying leaves, and the sound of a nearby rushing creek. I am also reveling in the bliss of how my life has turned out, how I've been able to put hundreds of miles between my life in the ultra-Orthodox community and my life way out here in West Virginia. The sense of contrast between life as a woodsman and life as a Brooklyn rabbi felt so freeing for me. Out here in the Allegheny Mountains I was safe from the watchful eyes and any accompanying judgments of the restrictive mindset I had long ago left behind. Finally, I was free from the inhibitions of the community in which I grew up, and from my own inhibitions, free to rabbi again but from where I was at as opposed to where I'd been reared.

I sat on the stoop a very long time, thankful for the guts that God gave me to break out from what had become for me increasingly restrictive, not so much from Jewish practice but from the heaviness I was experiencing around the way people were practicing Jewish. But here, deep in the woods, far from any Jewish community, let alone a remotely Orthodox one, I felt happy, liberated, uninhibited, totally freed up. They would never find me out here. I could live as I wished.

As I am sitting there lapping up the gifts of the moment, the phone rings. It's the warden at the men's facility in Morgantown.

"Rabbi, I've got a problem."

"Shoot."

"Well, it's a little more complicated than that. I've got two new Jewish inmates. They claim they can't pray with the rest of the guys for the upcoming holiday and that they need their own people to come down from New York to pray with them. They also claim that the kosher meals we provide for some of the other Jewish inmates is not kosher enough for them. Could you come over here tomorrow or some time soon to clear this up?"

The following morning I drive to Morgantown, two and a half hours, much of it spent dragging up hill behind coal trucks on roads that wind so sharply I am sure they were designed by a drunken driver for drunken drivers so that drunken drivers wouldn't look like they were driving drunk. I try hard to imagine what could possibly be the scenario I am about to encounter at the Prison Camp. Who are these characters? It's total nonsense that the kosher food they serve there would not be kosher enough for someone. Why they'd have to be Hasidim to have such extreme standards around kosher food, or to demand that a quorum of men be flown from New York for Yom Kippur services. So who were these new inmates?

When I arrive at the compound I am ushered into the warden's office immediately. And there, sitting across from the warden's desk in full Hasidic regalia are indeed two Hasidim, in long black coats, big black yarmulkas, long beards and earlocks. There, turning those all-so-familiar eyes at me, was the very community I never imagined would ever find me in the safe confines of my rural West Virginia lifestyle. Instantly, it occurs to me what it was that the Evil Inclination had been up to all this time behind my peaceful back. He had been busy getting these two guys into some unclean business trouble with the Feds so that they could be sentenced to a year at the Federal Prison Camp in—not New York, not Connecticut, not Pennsylvania, but—West Virginia! There they now sat, a half smile on each of their faces, the smile of the Evil One planted so smugly on two otherwise extremely pious Hasidic men.

"You're from Brooklyn, no?" one of them asks me.

"Sure he is," says the second guy, "I know his father. Winkler, yes?" .The warden sits up on his chair and leans over his desk toward me. "You know these guys?"

"No, sir, I don't know them at all. I mean it is possible they have met or heard of my father or of my family. Same community, sir. But, no, I never met these guys."

"Conflict of interest if you do," warns the warden, as puzzled by the strange scenario as I am.

The two Hasidim begin to plead with me in Yiddish that I convince the warden to allow them to bring in their own kosher food and to allow members of their community in New York to pray with them on *Yom Kippur*. I feel like the rabbis of the middle ages who were often called upon by their communities to petition dukes and bishops for the right to religious observances, or to cancel edicts aimed at their expulsion or destruction. The warden was now the duke and I the hapless spiritual leader of the peasant Jewish hamlet under the harsh rule of Jew-hating royalty.

"Sire, far be it from me to beseech thee on behalf of these two pitiful creatures, but, alas, I am so called to speak for them as they lack the words, and I, I am but a humble servant of thine excellency, kneeling at thine mercy, seeking thine benevolence for which I will be forever grateful with mine life and with the lives of mine children. As a mule beckons to its master, so doth I at this time beckon to thee to draw thy attention to the very peculiar circumstances of these two men who with me now stand before thee with our heads bowed."

"Speak then, and render thy words in brevity, for matters of state awaiteth mine tending."

"Aye, Sire. I shall indeed speak in brevity, mine supplication veiled by words that will not consume the time allotted your excellency in his precious lifetime, for all words are so measured that a man might have his moment to speak them, and thus is time likewise allotted for those whose ears might hear them so that they might take to heart what another man sayeth."

"Thou art wasting mine time, fool. Either thou speakest unto me thy request or I shall have thee thrown from the castle and cast into the moat, for perhaps as the crocodiles approach thee thou mayest then find the words thou seeketh, and in brevity."

"Truth speakest thou, Sire, and indeed I shall not cast into oblivion words fit for fodder, but shall in their stead resonate words fit for thine esteemed ears and heart."

"I shall indeed cut thine ears off and cast thine heart to the dogs if thou speaketh one more word not related to thy quest."

———————————

"These guys are the real McCoy, sir. Their standard of religious observance is very strict and demands a degree of meticulousness beyond what is required by conventional Orthodox Jewish law."

"I don't get it."

"You're Christian, sir?"

"Yes, I'm a Christian."

"You familiar with the Amish people?"

"Yes."

"Are Amish people Christians?"

"Yes, of course."

"Get it, sir?"

"Got it."

I arranged that the Hasids got shipments of kosher meals from a company approved by their community and that met its very high standards. The warden also approved the presence of fifteen Hasidim at the facility during Yom Kippur, flown in from New York at their own expense for the purpose of facilitating the new inmates' proper observance of Yom Kippur. All this time I heard both God and the Evil One laughing heartily while slapping one another on the back. It had been one helluva divine conspiracy. Whatever I was running away from seemed to always be one step behind me, or in this case, one step ahead of me waiting for my arrival in Morgantown. I would never be completely free from my past. It *schlepped* along with me every mile I put between myself and Brooklyn. Who was I kidding? I could have been living in the middle of Wyoming—better yet, the Arctic!—and a bus load of Hasidim would have found me sooner or later. It was inevitable and I might as well accept it.

That Yom Kippur, for the first time in the history of West Virginia, fifteen Hasidic Jews were walking up the hill toward a prison camp decked in prayer shawls and nearly causing multiple automobile collisions along the way as rednecked drivers of pickups did double and triple takes while swerving to avoid both the Hasidim and one another. It was a spectacle I shall never forget. I led a service with the other Jewish inmates in one room while the Hasidim prayed in a second room, and everybody was happy.

In the ensuing moons, however, each visit to the prison in Morgantown became a challenge to my theological evolution, as the two Hasids would constantly interrogate me, questioning my paradigm shift and reinstalling all of the guilt software I'd thought I'd long deleted from my program.

"You still keep kosher? What about *shabos?* We see you carrying on *shabos* when you come to the prison, and how could you play the guitar on *shabos?* Do you walk here when you visit the prison, or are you driving on *shabos?* How come you're not wearing a *yarmulka?* That woman who came with you on Yom Kippur, she's Jewish? She lives with you? How could you pray with her in the same room when you came for Yom Kippur? Are there Jews where you live? How could you live in a place where there are no other

Jews? Your parents must be grieving over you. How could you leave everything behind like that? Don't you know better? You who went to yeshiva all your life—how *could* you? Do you observe *any* thing at *all* anymore? Do you worship idols?"

I often prayed for the rehabilitation of prison inmates and for their subsequent release. For these two guys, however, I skipped the rehab part and just prayed that they be released without delay! It was more like asking someone to stop teasing you. God was playing with me and it was getting on my nerves. I realized that I had succeeded all these years in eluding all of the questions and challenges to my personal transformation process, questions still burning strong in the collective consciousness of the community I had fled. And now they had caught up with me in the guise of these two Hasids who unbeknownst to them, personified and embodied the very smoldering puzzlement and curiosity of the rest of that community around my defection.

And what was to be my response? Could I respond at all? Or would my response constitute an entirely different language to them since my mindset had by this juncture drifted as far apart from theirs as an Arctic iceberg from a South Pacific island. My responses, when I voiced them, clashed head on and ineffectually against the stalwart canyon walls of a deeply entrenched party-line mindset incapable or unwilling to sponge anything other than what smacked of itself. My responses were rejected with the spontaneity of, say, a rejected organ from an incompatible transplant recipient. My quoting to them from the very textual sources that graced their shelves at home was met not with contemplative consideration toward possibility but with admonishment for the crime of presuming that I had the authority to interpret or otherwise implement those teachings differently than the established party-line. The ancient Jewish tradition of challenging tradition had come to a complete standstill. This was a community whose religious zeal was fueled not by ancient wisdom but by collective paranoia around the illusory threat of a modern, technocratic culture to which ultra-traditionalists remained nonetheless both staunch opponents and devoted *com*ponents.

With each challenge and response I began to feel more and more isolated. Every visit with these two shadows of my own selfhood made it increasingly clear to me that I had evolved or mutated into some entirely different creature from the one that once suckled from the tits of the mainstream Jewish community. I began to understand more vividly the soul of the disparity reflected in the disputes between the ancient rabbis, between the spiritual teachers of the rural Galilean and Judean countrysides and the spiritual teachers of the more urban centers like Jerusalem and B'nai B'rak. These disputes between the masters, I now realized, stemmed not solely from differences in scriptural interpretations but from differences in lifestyles and mindsets.

I no longer thought the way these guys thought, no longer saw the world through those same eyes. Yet, while I could understand where they were coming from, having once been there myself, *they* could not begin to fathom where I was coming from, having never tasted of the forbidden fruit. Like every other mortal on the planet, they, too, *knew* the Evil Inclination, but, unlike most of us, had not yet ever *traveled* with him.

Within a year, the two Hasids were released and sent back to Brooklyn. With them went all of the residual doubts I had been harboring all these years around the rightness of my new life choice. Their challenges and questions, while at first painful and guilt-inducing, had ended up strengthening my convictions, spurring me deeper into my inescapable calling as a rabbi. After this year-long ordeal I felt like my now deceased master had re-ordained me yet a second time, this time not from his vision of me as a rabbi but from my own vision of me as a rabbi.

My original Jerusalem ordination had been lost in the Flood of '85, washed away with other papers down the Cacapon River. I had never bothered writing away for a second copy. It didn't feel at all important at the time, since I wasn't really planning to do any more rabbi'ing.

The loss of that paper appeared to me at the time as a cosmic sign that that way of rabbi'ing was gone gone gone, washed away by a latter-day Noahide deluge. But now I felt empowered again, self-affirmed, comfortable in the way I was living as a Jew and serving my people as a rabbi. I had finally confronted my shadow.

I did not question Orthodoxy, only its meaning and relevance for me personally and to others who find it a difficult option for them in their search for Jewish spiritual living and practice. I had been born, raised, and ordained in the Orthodox tradition, in the *yeshivish* community, and had spent eleven years teaching and inspiring non-Orthodox Jews to become Orthodox. I myself had been more orthodox than Moses, and I was so good at it that I could have easily turned a horse into a Sabbath-observant Jew in less than a week. Piece of cake. But at some point in my life, something far more expansive burned deep inside my heart and I wanted to know it. First I thought it was heartburn, but then I realized it wasn't nearly as bad as that. So I ended up spending the next two decades in the wilderness, doing my Jewish thing in a less orthodoxic, more *flex-idoxic*, manner that opened me in ways I'd never imagined. Still, I feel that every Jew should ideally start out Orthodox and then either remain there if it feels right for her or him, or move onward if it doesn't. Not *out*ward, *on*ward. The Orthodox tradition is extremely rich, and the background it gives one for understanding the soul of Judaism is priceless, (and so is the food).

For me, it felt important to examine the opinions and rulings in the Talmud and the *halachah* (Jewish religious law) that were *not* codified, that didn't make it into the "system" known as Orthodox Judaism. The more flexible attitude that I ended up adopting for myself was by no means any new invention of mine. Rather, it flows ever so freely through the Hebrew Scriptures, the Talmud, the Midrash, and the Codes, pumping eternal life through the heart of my people and its rich cosmology.

The Evil Inclination had cornered me into rediscovering what is the essence of being Jewish. He compelled me to go way way back to the ignored teachings of the very first Jew who lived some four thousand years ago: Harry Hochberg. Unable to make any sense of the available papyrus on Harry, I examined the teachings around the *second* first Jew, Abraham. I wanted to know what was the essence of being a follower of Abraham, and what hit me hardest was that his religion was awe at the mystery of Creator and Creation, and the fact that he called himself an *eev'ree* (Hebrew), meaning: "one who crosses over." Judaism, I realized, was a theology of boundary crossing. Since its birth, my people have relentlessly crossed the boundaries set by others, as well as its own boundaries—religious and otherwise. Virtually every generation, the Talmud demonstrates, challenged the religious, legal, and theological boundaries established for them by the previous generation. I mean, Jews walk into restaurants and are incapable of sticking to the menu. Non-Jewish restaurants now have a line on the bottom of each page of the menu that reads: "No substitutions allowed," clearly aimed at Jewish patrons who, even though they are not keeping kosher, are still *eev'reem.*

Judaism is a living path, a dynamic theology. Show me any legal ruling in the traditional Jewish codes and I will show you on the same page one or two or half a dozen sources who contest, qualify, reinterpret, or outright disagree with that ruling. I am a Jew. Give me a boundary, and I shall cross it.

> I will not be to my predecessors as a donkey, eternally hauling their books. I will explain their teachings and study their ways, but when my perception does not correspond to theirs … I will then decide according to what my own eyes are seeing, and will do so with legal confidence. For the Creator grants wisdom in every generation and in every period, and will not deny goodness to those who are sincere.
>
> **13th-century Rabbi Moshe ibn Nachmon in his introduction to *Sefer Hamitz'vot L'HaRambam***

Living in the wilderness, you see, helped me to see Judaism from outside the very narrow ways in which it had been defined for centuries through the lenses of cultures so deeply antithetical to anything remotely Jewish. The idea of religion itself is at best alien to aboriginal Judaism, a Judaism that had more to do with being than with doing, more to do with the *magic* of living than with the *protocols* of living.

[By the 18th century] religion in the new narrow sense borrowed from Christianity, became central to [the Jewish people's] understanding of what it meant to be Jewish, in ways in fact not traditional for them at all.

Traditionally, what we are accustomed to call religion had been [for the Jews] simply one aspect, though an important and central one, of a complete way of life. The laws regarding religion found their place among others governing business, social life, and the relationship of groups in the community to one another. Moving into an environment with a Christian conception of the place of religion in society, leaving behind the public and social aspects of the Torah, and adopting for themselves this new conception of religion, in subtle ways heavily Christianized even the most Orthodox of Jews.

Indeed, perhaps the effect on the most traditional Jews, the least recognized by themselves or by others, was the most profound, inasmuch as they now focused their intense loyalty to tradition on the details of religious observance that differentiated them from other Jews whose observance was laxer or more adjusted to modern conditions. Thus, their dedication to being Jewish became focused on religion to a degree Jews had hardly known before, and indeed was not

characteristic of the tradition. Today, even the most
conservative of all Jewish groups, the non-Zionist ultra-
Orthodox in Israel ... have been transformed, without themselves recognizing the fact, by this new Christian form of
religiousness into a style of Jewish existence unknown to
the original shapers of the tradition they revere.

**Professor William Nicholls in *Christian Antisemitism:
A History of Hate* [Jason Aronson:1995], pp. 287-288**

The longer I lived in the wilderness the more clear it became to
me that my ancestors were a tribal people that lived and practiced a
Judaism that in very few ways resembled the more urbanized Judaism
of today. Once upon a time my people enjoyed a relationship with
the earth that was more about spirituality than about commerce or
industry. Our visionaries came not from rabbinical seminaries and
academies of higher learning but from solitary walkabouts and vision
quests deep in the wilderness and far from the reaches of civilization. They were masters of sorcery and shamanism, dancing comfortably between the realms of spirit and matter, celebrating the
magic of the worlds around them and beyond them. They knew the
language of the trees, the grasses, the frogs, and the cicadas; the
thoughts of horses and sheep. They followed rivers to discover truths,
and climbed mountains to liberate their spirits. They journeyed
beyond their bodily limitations, brought back people from the dead,
healed the incurable, talked raging rivers into holding back their
rapids, turned pints into gallons, brought down the rains in times of
drought, walked through fire, even suspended the orbit of the earth
around the sun. And they did it all with a sense of humor.

Rabbi Chanina ben Dosa was walking along the way
when it began to rain. He prayed: "Master of the
Universe! The whole world benefits while Chanina
suffers?" Immediately the rains stopped. When he
arrived in his house he prayed: "Master of the

Universe! The whole world suffers while Chanina benefits?" Immediately the rains resumed.

◆§ Babylonian Talmud, *Yoma* 53b

My ancestors were powerful warriors and shamans, who, like the warriors and shamans of other aboriginal peoples, were swept under the rug by so-called civilization as it overtook an entire planet by force, subjugating spirituality and personal aliveness in the guise of "civilizing the primitives" and "saving souls."

And now I was coming back to *that* flavor of my people's ways. Living in the woods had brought me to a fresh and exciting encounter with the teachings of my own tradition that emerged from the inspiration that resonates most vividly in remote places. The rocks and the trees and the silence transformed me like no text of the Kabbalah could do.

Finale

During the heavily introspective Year of the Hasids, I had also busied myself with romancing Lakme, a process whose quality became increasingly refined by that very same process of self-discovery sparked by my encounters with the Hasids two weekends a month. The more certain I was of who I was and where I stood, the more serious I became in relationship to relationshiping. I made both a commitment and a commutement to Lakme during that year, driving to Chicago every other week to spend time getting to know her. In turn, she would come to West Virginia to spend time with me so that she could figure me out, or at the very least try.

In our romancing, as we became increasingly involved, I began feeling feelings I vowed never to feel again, like entertaining the notion of actually, maybe having a c-c-c-c-committed relationship with someone, or maybe even getting m-m-m-m-married again. But of course without any children in the picture. No kids, thank you very much. I'd done kids, been there, and now they were grown

up. And I wanted to be as freed up *in* a marriage or committed relationship as I was while being single.

"Before we get too involved, Lakme, I need you to really understand that I cannot, will not, ever live in a city or near one. I need to
live in the woods, way way way out in the boonies. And I need the
freedom to love other women if that happens to happen."

"I understand that about you, Gersh Song. And I need to say that
before we get too involved, I need you to really understand that I
need to have kids."

"Oh."

The idea of having kids was proposed by several other biological
tickers I had romanced in the past, and it had been so strong an
issue for me that whenever it was intimated red flags went up across
all my chakras and the relationship was terminated. In one instance,
the woman so wanted the relationship to survive that she changed
her mind about having children. That was a hard one to walk away
from: a woman who loved me so much that she was willing to relin-
quish her deepest wish. On the other hand, I felt at the time that it
would be so very wrong of me to cash in on her willingness to surrender what was clearly core to her. Plus she'd probably spend the
rest of our life together resenting me for it.

And here I was again, falling in love with a woman who—unlike
any other woman I'd ever dated—accorded me the freedom to exer-
cise the freedoms I'd been exercising, and who—unlike any other
woman I'd ever dated—made no attempts at changing me, at recre-
ating me in her own image. But she wanted kids. Two of them. And
what scared me most was that I found myself not saying my traditional No to the relationship. All I could muster was a weakly whispered Oh. Of course I shared my hesitations around the issue, why
it was I didn't want to do kids, how important my freedom was and
how deeply I feared losing that freedom by way of parental responsibility and duties.

"It's something that *I* want," she said, "and you *don't*. So I will
be the primary caretaker."

Phew. That felt so much better. I wouldn't have to deal with the kids, with feeding them, changing their diapers, putting them to sleep. I would be free to continue my life as is, unabated by the arrival of children. It felt better. I resolved to continue my romance with this Lakme woman as far as it would take us, even into marriage.

"Hello, Zalman?"

"Gersh?"

"Yup. How is everything?"

"Good. Thank God, all is well. Doing too much traveling, though. It's getting tiring."

"What kind of traveling? Been schlepping around to opticians again?"

"Not now, Gersh, not now. Tell me, what's going on with you these days?"

"Well, I have decided to get married."

"You're still going with Lakme?"

"Still."

"Gersh, be careful. You know that she wants children, don't you?"

"I know."

"Gersh, listen. It's clear that you don't want to do kids, so you better think this one through carefully."

"I have thought it through and we've discussed it thoroughly. She assured me that she'll be the primary caretaker."

There was a pause for what seemed to be a long period of time.

"Gersh."

"Yes, Zalman?"

"*Azoi hoben zey mir oich arein gefurt* [Yiddish: That's how they led me into it, too]."

And thus was I sacrificed on the altar of the Goddess, swept lock stock'n'barrel into marriage with children, neither of which I imagined I would ever want to do again. We were married by Zalman at Mount Eden, a wild retreat center and farm in western New Jersey, and lived happily ever after. As for the kid that eventually came into our lives—well, primary caretaker my ass. The moment Aharonit was born I was so totally smitten I *relished* my time to play with her or feed her or change her diapers or put her to sleep.

The child waited patiently for more than two years, though, before descending upon us, enabling her future parents to further solidify their relationship. In the meantime, Lakme accompanied me on some of my circuits, especially my visits to the women's prison in Alderson. She also expressed concern over raising our child in pretty much a uni-cultural region, preferring instead a multi-racial, multi-cultural living situation such as, say, New Mexico. So we began to study and dream about New Mexico. Now that my kids were grown up and dating, I felt the resurrection of my original dream of living in the west. I had my heart set on Wyoming, but New Mexico would do so long as we lived in the sticks.

At the women's prison, our program was drawing inmates not solely from the modest Jewish population there but also from the Rastafarian and Native American inmate populations. Somehow they felt more comfortable with the Jewish circle than with some of the other available options, and especially the Native American women expressed to us time and again how similar were our ways with theirs, our cosmology with their cosmology, our ways of chanting and theirs. So during our first scouting tour of New Mexico I bought a tape of Native American medicine songs by this Choctaw medicine carrier named David Carson, and gifted it to the Native American women at Alderson. They loved the tape so much I was moved to write to this Carson fellow, thanking him for inspiring women behind bars.

He wrote back, and then sent me a bunch of free *Medicine Cards* packages that he had co-authored, cards with pictures of animals, accompanied by a book about the medicine of each of them. I distributed the packages to the Native American inmates and thus began a sweet correspondence back and forth between myself and David Carson, who I discovered soon enough, dwelled in New Mexico.

In the summer of 1992, we rented a truck and moved to New Mexico, renting a cabin in the woods north of Taos while we drove all around the state in search of a place we'd want to call home. We didn't have a clue of where to begin, but David had sent us some phone numbers of friends of his whom he felt would help us find our initial abode. And they did. David was out of the country when we relocated, doing workshops in Russia and hanging with Siberian shamans on the other side of the planet. When he finally returned, he located us through his friends and called to say hello.

Hello.

"So David, when can we finally meet face to face?"

"Well, Nina and I are getting married next Sunday night. Why don't you and Lakme come to the wedding?"

"We'd be delighted!"

"Oh, that reminds me, Gershon, I have a question for you."

"I'm listening."

"Is it okay for a rabbi to do a wedding ceremony for an injun?"

"David, in all of my many years of studies of the Hebrew scriptures, the Talmud, or the Codes of Jewish Law, I have never ever come upon a prohibition against a rabbi doing a ceremony for an injun."

"Well, would you honor us by doing the ceremony?"

That's how I first met David Carson. I did his wedding. And at the ceremony I was introduced to other Native Americans who were acquaintances of David. And the more we dialogued then and in the following years, the more we came to discover how much our traditions and cosmologies shared in common. I grew so close to David and felt so deep a connection from my Judaism to his Native Americanism that one day while we sat on his porch together looking out at the endless mesas and colorful horizons of New Mexico, I turned to him and asked what it would take for us to become blood brothers. You know, like in the movies.

"Well," he drawled, his ancient eyes fixated on the setting sun, "in my tradition we would cut some flesh from our arms, yours and mine, and then hang the flesh up on a tree in a buckskin medicine pouch."

There was a pause for what seemed to be a long period of time. I patted him on his shoulder, joined him in watching the setting sun, and said: "Well, maybe I could be your cousin. Twice removed, that is, just to be on the safe side."

Soon the dialogue between Judaism and Native America expanded, and the idea was born of conducting a wilderness spirituality retreat that featured the spirit wisdom and earth ceremonies of both traditions, taught by teachers indigenous to each. Dubbed "Lighting the Story Fires Within," the retreat ultimately inspired "Jewish Shamanism" retreats and, more recently, "Jewish Shamanic Healing" workshops that I co-teach with colleague Miriam Maron, a spiritual healer and Jewish song/chant album artist (*Wings of Light* and *Light Out of Darkness*). Other retreats followed as well in response to requests from Jewish communities across the USA, Canada, Europe, and Israel, to share the restoration of aboriginal Jewish wisdom and the art of dancing *with*—rather than fighting *against*—the Evil Inclination.

In 1997, with the support of a Jewish elder, Robert A. Levin, and a handful of others whose lives were transformed through these teachings, eighty-four acres of scenic New Mexico wilderness were purchased, and the Walking Stick Foundation was born. The name "Walking Stick" was inspired by our intention of sharing ancient Jewish and other earth-based wisdom for us to lean on while biding our time on earth.

And so, at the crescendo of my journey I am left to a life of serenity, good health, good family life, deep joyfulness, sound lovingness, real-time spirituality, and not a single complaint.

Well, not exactly. I do have one complaint. The IRS won't accept the Evil Inclination as an additional dependent.

Epilogue

On the eve of January 31, 1994, I suffered a major stroke. The initial symptoms were that I lost all feeling on my left side from my shoulders down to my toes and was unable to move my left limbs. Also, I was only able to think in Lithuanian Yiddish. Being a man, I didn't want to wake my wife for fear of disturbing her peaceful sleep for something as trivial as a stroke. Actually, I had no clue what a stroke was, let alone its symptoms, and simply assumed that I was slowly dying, one limb at a time. And why bother waking up Lakme when I'm dying? I mean, like, give me a break—I couldn't think of any last words worth waking someone up for. Plus—even if I *could* think of some fancy last words, she wouldn't have understood the Yiddish anyhow. So I decided to let it ride until morning since there wasn't much Lakme could have done about it anyway. You know, dead is dead, right? Period. Finito. To quote a well-known Gentile cartoon character: *Bedebeebedebee dat's all, folks!* Right? So I drifted off to what I presumed was going to be death.

———————————

"Name?"

It was the Angel of Death, bathed in a white light that flickered on and off. He kept shaking himself to keep it lit but to no avail. "Name?" he repeated, leafing through some papers on a celestial clipboard.

"Oh. Uh . . . Gershon Winkler."

"Hmmmm. Don't see you here. Mother's maiden name?"

"Broda."

"Ah! Here you are. They had you under your first name. They always do this to me. Okay. Your soul, please?"

"My what?"

"Your soul, pin head, your SOUL! Hand it over. Here's your receipt."

"I haven't a clue *where* my soul is. I mean, like I don't know what part of me is my soul, if you know what I mean."

"Great. This I *need:* another Aquarian. Listen, *boytchik*, I haven't got the energy for this. I'll catch you some other time."

"You mean I'm not gonna be dead?"

"I don't think you're ready."

"Hey, can I at least see my dead relatives before I go? I never met my grandfathers, you know. And . . . and my teacher, the old man with the long white beard, Reb Eliezer, can I see him? What about Moses, Abraham, Deborah, Samson? Better yet . . . Delilah?!"

"Listen my eager friend. If I let you see a few, you will have to see them all."

"Meaning what? I mean, like what's so bad about that? You think I'm afraid to see Haman and Hitler and Stalin and those kinds of folks?"

"How's about your creditors, *boytchik?*"

"I'm outta here."

———————

And so I woke up early the next morning, still breathing, and still completely numb on my entire left side excluding my neck and up. I slowly turned to Lakme who was yawning and stretching, and gently broke the news. Before I could finish explaining my symptoms she was on the phone with Dick Kozoll, the only local physician, a nice Jewish boy from Chicago who'd come way out here over two decades ago to complete his residency and never left. Dick instructed Lakme to bring me to his clinic in the nearby village of Cuba, where he was in the middle of dealing with another emergency. Lakme helped me dress, button my shirt, tie my boots, and half-carried my half-limp body to the car. It was snowing that morning. At the clinic, Dr. Kozoll recognized the symptoms immediately, took my blood pressure to confirm his diagnosis, and discussed with Lakme the options of waiting for a chopper to arrive from the nearest hospital some 85 miles away or her driving me there. Lakme wasted no time mustering her Chicago winter driv-

ing skills and drove me speedily through the snowstorm to Albuquerque, braving frozen tumbleweeds, slippery roadways and blind-
ing snowflakes.

I spent five days at Presbyterian Hospital in Albuquerque where
they had me down as "Christian." At first I thought of informing them
that I was Jewish, but then I figured I'd leave the matter alone. After
all, it allowed me some freedom in behaving any damn way I
pleased, because whatever I'd do or say, they wouldn't blame it on
the Jews.

Lakme remained at my side throughout my stay at the hospital
and kept my spirits afloat. I was also visited every other day by Rabbi
Lynn Gottlieb who had us both bent over in deep belly laughter
with her wild sense of humor. When she noticed that I couldn't move
my left hand, she cried: "Oy! The stroke has affected your speech, too!
You can only talk with *one hand!*" Needless to say, the laughter shot
up my blood pressure to dangerously high degrees causing a series
of seventeen consecutive strokes and shattering the intravenous bottles. I was also visited by David Carson, my Choctaw friend, and his
buddy Kam Night Chase, a Lakota Sun Dance Chief who wasted no
time piercing my chest and suspending me from the ceiling fan. They
also smudged me with sage, which then set off smoke alarms and
sent nurses, doctors, and orderlies scurrying about, and heart pac-
ers going off everywhere.

I was also visited in the middle of the night by a delegation of
schmelves (Jewish elves) who convinced me that the stroke was a
punishment for not believing that schmelves actually exist. They
then left me with an outdated Hebrew calendar decorated with
blurry pictures of biblical characters with their left sides missing.
When I protested and struggled to reach for the nurse-call button,
they simply shrugged and told me to chalk it up to one more punishment. "And what, pray tell, would that be for?" I shouted, my
diastolic shooting up to 188. "For believing for one moment that
you were being punished!" they yelled back and ran off chuckling
to themselves.

The stroke was not supposed to have happened to me. I was doing sixty-five push-ups every morning, hiking two to three miles minimum daily through rugged mountain country, and didn't eat fatty foods or much salt. But I've been teaching about how there are no guarantees in life, and I guess I like to practice what I preach. So there. And someone told me that shamans receive their initiation by having strokes. Especially shamans with high blood pressure. So there. And hypertension runs in my family, so I should have been monitoring my blood pressure all these years even though I hadn't gotten sick or needed a doctor. So let that be a warning to some of you. And you know who you are.

The hospital transferred me to a rehabilitation center where they tried teaching me how to walk again, and to regenerate the use of my left arms and hands. Of course, I would clown around in my typical slapstick way at every opportunity, sending the therapists to their clipboards for notations. At one point while I was *putzing* around, the chief therapist approached Lakme to console her, telling her not to worry, explaining very delicately that her husband's strange and impulsive behavior was most probably due to the effect that the stroke had on the right side of the brain. Lakme listened attentively and then replied: "But this is exactly how he *always* behaves."

Longing for the mountains and the wilderness, I quit the rehab thing after a few weeks and decided to heal by continuing to hike my wilderness environment back home, complete with a walker and knee and elbow pads. Lakme added a crash helmet. I also practiced riding one-legged up and down the dirt road on a bike, falling and getting up, falling and getting up. After every outing I would return home with fresh bruises from frequent falls over sharp rocks, fallen trees, protruding roots, cacti, and from tripping over my crash helmet. While the wide array of cuts and bruises looked and felt bad, I was experiencing more and more restoration of feelings in my body, and the miracle of nerve regeneration. Soon I was off the walker and hiking with a walking stick. But the fine-tuning of sensation and muscle control in my fingers and toes, and of my balance in general, seemed hopeless or at the very best a long way off.

I was determined not to label this stroke as a stroke or as anything that couldn't be fixed or transformed in some way. I remember sitting on a ledge overlooking the Nacimiento peaks, talking to the Creator about how important it was for me to be able to continue walking this magical planet, smelling her alluring aromas, and seeing her awesome beauty. "Whatever you allow to happen to me, do not allow my legs to falter, or my vision to fade." I remember rising in defiance of my weak balance and committing to the continuance of my life flow, my life vision, my life walk, in spite of the debilitating effects of the stroke, and then falling flat on my back as I turned and walked into an equally determined Ponderosa Pine.

How preposterous, I kept thinking, all this stuff about the shaman becoming initiated through happenings like strokes. Here I was, stricken with stroke, and nothing had changed in my mostly platonic relationship with shamanism. I'd been teaching the Jewish sources for a once-shamanic tradition in Judaism, but had no live-wire connection with any of it. It was something of the distant past before Jews and Judaism became integrated into the Occident. So nothing had changed for me around this. All that had changed was that I was having an extremely difficult time walking, buttoning my shirt, tying my boots, bathing, and, sadly, I could no longer play the guitar. The guitar had for decades been an important instrument for me since music and singing was an integral component of the way in which I was accustomed to teaching.

On my first "gig" after the stroke, I found myself in deep emotional pain over not being able to play the guitar anymore, to sing as I used to, as part of my teaching repertoire. It felt kind of like having an ice cream cone that had no ice cream in it. Or like drinking a tall glass of unsweetened lemonade. Or like dreaming that you're having great sex with a total stranger who then gives you their phone number and then you wake up with the realization that they'd neglected to give you the area code.

Anyway, I had a stroke, and it didn't make me any more a shaman than I already wasn't.

Then one day, while stumbling through the mountains, I tripped over a large stone and fell into some scrub oak. I slowly wiggled my way out of the brush, but couldn't get up because I'd hit my left leg on the stone as I fell. The impact paralyzed my movement in the leg, its fledgling nerves still unaccustomed to trauma.

So I just sat there, waiting patiently for the leg to work again. Stuck, I listened to the rhythm of the crickets, and the singing of the birds. Together they reminded me of the sound of one of my people's ancient musical instruments: the tambourine. I recalled the verse from the Book of Job: "Ask now of the earth and she shall inform you; of the beasts of the field and they shall guide you; of the birds of the sky and they shall teach you; of the fishes of the sea and they shall tell it to you" (Job 12:7-9).

Before my next teaching event, I purchased a tambourine and used my right hand to slap it rhythmically against my thigh, then rattle it in the air. It wasn't the same as playing the guitar; neither was the quality of stirring that it elicited deep within me, a stirring that moved me to chant instead of sing, and slowly I began to recover ancient Hebraic and Aramaic chants that I'd learned years ago and had since neglected. The chants moved not only me but those who came to hear me teach. The guitar had been entertaining, while the tambourine and the chants it inspired were transformative.

Years later, while teaching in the Judean Desert in Israel, I would be introduced to the soul-stirring sound of yet another of my people's ancient instruments, the drum. I had only been exposed to Native American drumming, and to Celtic drumming, and to Rock'n Roll drumming. The deep, hollow, haunting sound of desert drumming by Jews returning to their ancient roots joined by Bedouins frequenting our Tent of Gathering, brought me home to the drum. After several years of searching for just the right drum, I finally found one and we have been inseparable since, leading people in sacred dance, chant, journeying, and healing.

Epilogue

By 2003, I had regained 95% of my capacity to walk (with no hiking stick), run, climb, and even play a few chords on the guitar. I can easily attribute my remarkable recovery to the shamanic healing that occurred through various personal life-changing experiences with the earth, the trees, the drum, the chant . . . but truth be told, I think it was more the kid. Face it, I had to chase this kid around, pick her up, walk with her, climb rocks with her, run her obstacle course daily replete with Legos and other toys strewn across the floor—from her first through her eighth year at this writing (and still going). I firmly believe that the surest cure for stroke victims is to have a kid. Aharonit was conceived right after the stroke, and has to this day done more toward my healing than could the finest rehab facility worldwide.

The stroke, I feel, challenged me to become more a dad than a shaman.

Final Epilogue (for real)

People think I am strange because I spend more time with schmelves (Jewish elves) than with mortals. They also think I'm strange because I live so remote. My nearest neighbor is a mile and a half, and only in one direction. The fact is I am extremely strange. That is the meaning of my name: *ger'shon*, ancient Hebrew for "ever-transforming stranger" or "stranger over there." Exactly over where, no one knows. Not even I. Not even my mother, who named me after her father who named her after his mother who named him from a bowl of kosher alphabet soup.

I never wanted to be a rabbi. The elder with the white beard who initiated me back in Jerusalem, the late Rabbi Eliezer Benseon, kept insisting I needed to become a rabbi. And I kept insisting I needed to become a writer. In the end, I became both a rabbi *and* a writer. In fact, I became one of the most dynamic and charismatic Jewish teachers in the world today. Maybe even in the Middle East. I became acutely aware of my greatness when I won entry into "Who's Who

In Humility" last year. They disqualified me this year on a minor technicality. I had re-applied. Picky, picky, picky.

Even though I am the greatest rabbi who ever lived to write about it, a lot of people are very alienated by me. They feel I joke around too much, I am not reverent enough, and when they attend my classes or workshops they don't know when to take me seriously, how to discern between the learning and the funning. Truth is, I don't know the difference either. For me, the funning is as much the learning as is the learning the funning.

There is not a religious service or workshop that I conduct that does not have two or three people actually storm out in a huff, while the rest of the crowd remains helplessly bent over in deep belly-laughter and absorbing more learning than they ever would have from a more serious version of myself. The truth is, Judaism is a very funny religion. If it weren't, I'd have converted to something else long ago. Too many of us take life too seriously, and it is my job to change that. In fact, some people have even encouraged me to apply for the role of Messiah, which I've done. I haven't heard back yet.

Being a rabbi and living some 2,000 miles from the Second-Avenue Deli has been both a challenge and an adventure. Here in the boonies I can do what I want. Even God can't see me because there are too many ridges and trees in the way. I have lived in these remote regions since 1982 and could never ever return to urban life. I am spoiled. Here, in betwixt my circuit riding and teaching gigs around the country, I am just another cowboy, another hillbilly, another redneck. I sport teeth with missing fillings and dentures and wear dirty jeans and smelly shirts. To pick up my mail, I have to drive nine bumpy miles into town (population 760) in an old beat-up pick-up truck full of molding alfalfa, a bent screw driver, some rusty piping, some helplessly tangled baling twine, and a heap of outdated Jewish calendars. I use filthy language with the locals, listen politely to dirty jokes at the village dump, help neighboring ranchers round up their strays and load up their hay bales, and get invited to ceremonial dances by the local Indians.

Epilogue

If I am asked what has been my craziest, wildest, most unusual experience in my travels with the Evil Inclination, I fluctuate between the time I rented a cabin in the Colorado Rockies from that Jew-hating white supremacist to the time I did a wedding and the groom's aunt, who was from Chicago, didn't believe I was a real rabbi. "Tell me the truth," she insisted after the ceremony. "You're not a *real* rabbi, are you? I won't tell anybody. You're an actor, right? I know my nephew." I nodded in agreement and watched her whisper the Truth into the ears of all the relatives from his side. They're divorced now.

As for the white supremacist, who, as you know, I first encountered in a saloon in a rural dirt road town in Colorado—he and I became the best of friends and he never again told racial jokes, at least not in my presence. We became so close I even offered to circumcise him. For my wedding present, he sent me a circular saw blade on which he'd painted a snowy mountain scene with my cabin in it, and an accompanying note suggesting I hang it on the wall over the head of my bed.

Then there was the time I had to track down a bona fide Voodoo priestess at the request of a Hassidic rabbi in Brooklyn. Turns out that two of his constituents believed themselves to have been cursed Voodoo-style by some Puerto Ricans whom they'd alienated. They journeyed from Kabbalist to Kabbalist for advice until one elderly rabbi in Israel told them that the only way to remove the spell was to find a Voodoo priestess to do it. So they informed their rabbi in Brooklyn who called others who called others who called others until someone mentioned this strange rabbi prancing about in the sticks of northern New Mexico practicing Jewish Shamanism and sticking pins in *mezuzahs*. Surely, I ought to know some Voodoo people.

I didn't. But I knew how to find some. None of them lived in New York, though, so I learned some Voodoo rites over the phone from an elder priest in Miami who then sent me all kinds of stuff like powdered egg shells and exotic flower extracts, and directed me to do a ritual for the hapless pair in Brooklyn on my next trip east.

I'd forgotten to inform my wife about the pending arrival of the strange concoction, so we ended up having it for dinner one night. Not bad, actually.

Otherwise nothing much has happened with me as a rabbi, unless you count my befriending a Palestinian Muslim Sheikh in a small West Bank village and then flying him to the states on a peace tour that included his participation in a traditional Lakota Sun Dance in the Nevada desert. (He returned home just in time for the onset of the second Intifada.) Or the time I picked up a young man and woman hitchhiking on a remote country road in the Colorado Rockies and drove them 60 miles to their cabin, only to discover the following morning that they were wanted for armed robbery and attempted murder.

Otherwise, my life as a rabbi has been pretty much uneventful. And as for the Evil Inclination, we still travel together from time to time, only we're slowly drifting apart, as my attention has lately been diverted toward some very special women that he'd gotten me involved with.

Damn. That circular saw just fell off the wall again.